WORD OF GOD, SONG OF LOVE

*

WORD OF GOD, SONG OF LOVE

✳

A Commentary on the Song of Songs

Raymond Jacques Tournay, O.P.

Translated by J. Edward Crowley

PAULIST PRESS

New York, NY/Mahwah, NJ

This book is a translation of *Quand Dieu parle aux hommes le langage de l'amour* (Cahiers de la Revue Biblique 21) by Raymond Jacques Tournay, O.P., published by J. Gabalda et Cⁱᵉ, Paris: 1982.

Book design by Ellen Whitney.

Library of Congress Cataloging-in-Publication Data

Tournay, Raymond Jacques, 1912–
    [Quand Dieu parle aux hommes le langage de l'amour. English]
    Word of God, song of love : a commentary on the Song of songs /
Raymond Jacques Tournay ; translated by J. Edward Crowley.
        p.   cm.
    Bibliography: p.
    Includes indexes.
    ISBN 0-8091-3007-6 (pbk.)
    1. Bible. O.T. Song of Solomon—Criticism, interpretation, etc.
I. Bible. O.T. Song of Solomon. English. 1988.   II. Title.
BS1485.2.T6813 1988
223'.906—dc19   88-23572
                                                                              CIP

Published by Paulist Press
997 Macarthur Boulevard
Mahwah, New Jersey 07430

Printed and bound in the
United States of America

CONTENTS

PREFACE

*I*n 1967 I published a small book, *Le Cantique des Cantiques, Édition abrégée* (Éditions du Cerf, Paris), in which, with the assistance of Mlle Miriam Nicolaÿ, I gave a summary of André Robert's major commentary, a posthumous work which had been brought out under my supervision in 1963 (Éditions Gabalda, Paris). In the 1967 work I followed the general interpretation developed in the Robert volume. But this to my mind was only one step in the long journey toward a better understanding of the Song of Songs.

After years of reflection and teaching and spurred on by recent works, such as the imposing commentary of Marvin Pope in the *Anchor Bible* series (1977), I decided to take up anew the complete exegesis of the Song. A number of articles had already allowed me to propose some new interpretations. These to be sure were not retractions, as some commentators made them out to be, but an attempt at a more rigorous and coherent general line of interpretation, capable of organically fitting in the two main tendencies in modern exegesis of the Song: one emphasizing eroticism and the other, allegory. To me it seems possible to establish scientifically from the text itself a better balance in the light of the history of the people of Israel and especially of the evolution of their faith in messianism.

The most fruitful hermeneutical principle here seems to me to be that of double meaning (in English there is even the phrase "double entendre"), already made use of, I think, by whoever was responsible for the definitive edition of the Song of Songs. This highly poetical booklet resists any attempt at segmentation ("atomization"); in its present canonical biblical state it presents itself as an integral part of the Old Testament. The reading which

I propose seeks to integrate two levels which, it seems to me, would be fruitless to reduce to mere opposites, when they seem rather to be correlative.

The mystery of human love is inseparable from that of Divine Love of which it constitutes the sign and symbol. This poem, the Song of Songs, is a vibrant witness to this, ever valid and more than ever indispensable to people of our time.

R. J. Tournay, O.P.

Jerusalem, Christmas 1981

École Biblique et Archéologique Française

TRANSLATOR'S NOTE

A s in the French edition, the Hebrew personal name of the God of Israel is transliterated by the consonants YHWH. The reader may substitute the traditional translation "the Lord."

All references to biblical texts are based on the verse numbering of the Massoretic text. This is especially to be noted in references to the psalms where there is often considerable variation in verse numbering.

Hebrew words are frequently included in transliteration so that the reader who does not know Hebrew may appreciate the sound and shape of some of the Song's more significant words and phrases. This is especially necessary to help recognize the abundance of significant assonances, alliteration and paronomasia in the Song, as well as allusions important for its interpretation. However, the translation is also always indicated. The system of transliteration is that followed in "Instructions for Contributors" in *Journal of Biblical Literature* 95 (1976), p. 334 and *The Catholic Biblical Quarterly* 38 (1976), nn. 23–25.

In the translation of the Song of Songs I tried to emulate Père Tournay's faithful rendering of the Hebrew text; although I carefully followed his French translation, at all times I had the original text in view. The translation of both the Song and the rest of the book was done in consultation with Père Tournay and any deviation from the French text was approved or sometimes suggested by him.

This readiness in regard to revision is evident too in his approach to the exegesis of the Song, which he has described as a long journey toward a better understanding of the Song of Songs (Preface). At the present stage of his research he is satisfied with showing that a messianic reading of the Song is possible. By using

3

"double meaning" as a hermeneutical principle, he discovers allusions that bring out the hidden riches of the Song as well as of other texts, especially postexilic ones. When the Song is studied against the background of Chronicles, Zechariah 9–14, etc., it can be seen that the idealized remembrance of Solomon in the postexilic community had given rise to the hope in a future peaceful king and the realization of the promises of the Covenant. The daughter of Zion longs for that new Solomon, the new manifestation of divine love for the restored community. But the Song also sings of the love of Solomon and the daughter of Pharaoh, human love that mirrors the love of God for people. Deeper meanings are discovered without any recourse to the excesses of allegory.

Tournay's emphasis on double entendre as a hermeneutical principle opens the way to new insights on the biblical message. Those involved in literary study beyond the Bible are often more appreciative of this dimension. Robert Alter[1] refers to it in his chapter on the Song of Songs entitled "The Garden of Metaphor." A special mention of double entendre is also made by Dr. Janet K. Larson,[2] a professor of English, in a review of Canadian novelist and poet Margaret Atwood's *The Handmaid's Tale:* "Like biblical Hebrew, Atwood's witty prose is thick with *double entendre* and allusion, including hidden puns whose meanings dawn on us only later. . . . "

I wish to thank Père Tournay for agreeing to this translation and for his promptness in answering my letters and my questions as I prepared the translation. I wish to thank too my wife, Dr. Pamela J. Milne, for her advice on the translation as well as for being both computer tutor and trouble-shooter for the word processing of this book.

[1] *The Art of Biblical Poetry* (New York, Basic Books, Inc., 1985), pp. 185–203.

[2] "Margaret Atwood's Testaments: Resisting the Gilead Within," *The Christian Century* 104 (May 20–27, 1987), pp. 496–98.

ABBREVIATIONS

AnBib	Analecta biblica
ANEP	*Ancient Near East in Pictures*
ANET	*Ancient Near Eastern Texts*
AOAT	Alter Orient und Altes Testament
ASTI	*Annual of the Swedish Theological Institute*
BA	*Biblical Archaeologist*
BASOR	*Bulletin of the American Schools of Oriental Research*
BASP	*Bulletin of the American Society of Papyrologists*
BBB	Bonner biblische Beiträge
BdJ	*La Bible de Jérusalem*
BETL	Bibliotheca ephemeridum theologicarum lovaniensium
Bib	*Biblica*
BKAT	Biblischer Kommentar: Altes Testament
BTB	*Biblical Theology Bulletin*
BWANT	Beiträge zur Wissenschaft vom Alten und Neuen Testament
BZ	*Biblische Zeitschrift*
BZAW	Beihefte zur *ZAW*
CBQ	*Catholic Biblical Quarterly*
CEg	*Chronique d'Égypte*
DBSup	*Dictionnaire de la Bible, Supplément*
ETL	*Ephemerides theologicae lovanienses*
FRLANT	Forschungen zur Religion und Literatur des Alten und Neun Testaments

HAT	Handbuch zum Alten Testament
HTR	*Harvard Theological Review*
HUCA	*Hebrew Union College Annual*
IEJ	*Israel Exploration Journal*
JA	*Journal asiatique*
JAOS	*Journal of the American Oriental Society*
JB	*Jerusalem Bible*
JBL	*Journal of Biblical Literature*
JEA	*Journal of Egyptian Archaeology*
JNES	*Journal of Near Eastern Studies*
JOÜON	JOÜON, *Grammaire de l'hébreu biblique*, 2nd edit., Rome, 1947
JPOS	*Journal of the Palestine Oriental Society*
JSOT	*Journal for the Study of the Old Testament*
JSS	*Journal of Semitic Studies*
JTS NS	*Journal of Theological Studies, New Series*
KB	KOEHLER and BAUMGARTNER, *Lexicon in VT libros*
LAPO	Littératures anciennes du Proche-Orient
LXX	Septuagint
LYS	D. LYS, *Le plus beau chant de la création* (Lectio Divina 51)
MAD	*Materials for the Assyrian Dictionary*, Oriental Institute, Univ. of Chicago (also *CAD*)
MT	Massoretic Text
NAB	*New American Bible*
NIV	*New International Version*
OBO	Orbis Biblicus et Orientalis
Or	*Orientalia*
PEQ	*Palestine Exploration Quarterly*

POPE	M. POPE, *Song of Songs* (Anchor Bible 7C), New York, 1977
RB	*Revue biblique*
REJ	*Revue des études juives*
RevQ	*Revue de Qumran*
RevScRel	*Revue des sciences religieuses*
RHR	*Revue de l'histoire des religions*
ROBERT-TOURNAY	A. ROBERT and R. TOURNAY, *Le Cantique des Cantiques* (Études Bibliques), Paris, 1963
RSR	*Recherches de science religieuse*
RSV	*Revised Standard Version*
SBL DS	Society of Biblical Literature, Dissertation Series
TDNT	*Theological Dictionary of the New Testament*
TOB	*Traduction oecuménique de la Bible, Ancien Testament*, Paris, 1974
ThQ	*Theologische Quartalschrift*
UF	*Ugarit-Forschungen*
VT	*Vetus Testamentum*
VTSup	Vetus Testamentum, Supplements
WZKM	*Wiener Zeitschrift für die Kunde des Morgenlandes*
ZAW	*Zeitschrift für die alttestamentliche Wissenschaft*
ZDPV	*Zeitschrift des deutschen Palästina-Vereins*
ZKTh	*Zeitschrift für katholische Theologie*
ZThK	*Zeitschrift für Theologie und Kirche*

THE SONG OF SONGS

Title

Chapter I

1. The Song of Songs, by Solomon

Prologue

SHE

2. Let him kiss me with the kisses of his mouth,
   for more delicious than wine are your caresses.
3. As for fragrance, your perfumes are a delight;
   a delicate perfume is your name;
   this is why the maidens love you.
4. Draw me after you, let us run;
   the King shows me to his room.
   Let us rejoice, let us make merry because of you;
   we will celebrate your caresses more than wine;
   how rightly do they love you.

First Poem

SHE

5. I am browned, but beautiful,
   daughters of Jerusalem,

like the tents of Kedar,
like the pavilions of Salma.[1]

6. Do not stare at my darkened skin;
    it is the sun that has burned me.
    My mother's sons took out their anger on me:
    they made me take care of the vineyards;
    my own vineyard I did not guard.

7. Tell me then, you whom my heart loves:
    Where you pasture your flock,
    where you rest them at mid-day?
    That I may no longer be a wanderer [2]
    by the flocks of your companions!

CHORUS

8. If you do not know, O most beautiful of women,
    follow the tracks of the flock,
    and take your young goats to graze
    near the shelters of the shepherds.

HE

9.   To my mare, among Pharaoh's chariots,
     I would compare you, my love.
10. Your cheeks are lovely between the pendants
     and your neck within the garlands.
11. We will make pendants of gold for you
     and ornaments of silver.

---

[1] *Salma*, correction; *Solomon*, MT.

[2] "Wanderer," *keto'iyyâ*, correction; "veiled," MT. See p. 123, n. 26.

SHE

12.   While the King is on his couch,
      my nard gives forth its fragrance.
13.   My beloved, for me, is a sachet of myrrh;
      he passes the night between my breasts.
14.   My beloved, for me, is a cluster of henna
      in the vineyards of En Gedi.

HE

15.   How beautiful you are, my love,
      how beautiful you are!
      Your eyes are doves.

SHE

16.   How beautiful you are, my beloved,
      how graceful.
      Our bed is of green leaves alone.
17.   The beams of our dwelling are of cedar,
      our ceiling, of cypresses.

Chapter II

SHE

1.   I am the narcissus of Sharon,
     the lily of the valleys.

HE

2.   Like the lily among the thistles,
     so is my love among the young women.

SHE

3. Like an apple tree among the trees of the forest,
   so is my beloved among the young men.
   In his shade which I so desire I sat
   and his fruit is sweet to my palate.

4. He brings me to his wine nook,
   and his banner for me is Love.

5. Strengthen me with raisin cakes,
   refresh me with apples,
   for I am love-sick.

6. His left hand is under my head,
   and his right embraces me.

7. I put you under oath, daughters of Jerusalem,
   by the gazelles, by the wild does,
   do not rouse, do not awaken Love
   before it so desires.

Second Poem

SHE

8. I hear my beloved.
   Look, he is coming,
   leaping on the mountains,
   bounding on the hills.

9. My beloved is like a gazelle,
   like a young fawn.
   Look, there he is standing
   behind our wall.

He is peeking in the window,
he is peering through the lattice.

10. My beloved calls out to me
    and he says to me:
    "Get up, my love,
    my beautiful one, and come away!
11. For see, winter is past,
    the rains are over and gone.
12. All over the land flowers are appearing;
    the time for pruning has come,
    and the cooing of the turtle-dove
    is heard in our land.
13. The fig tree is forming its first fruits,
    and the plants in bud give forth a sweet smell.
    Get up, my love,
    my beautiful one, and come away!
14. My dove, in the hollow of the rock,
    in the hidden places of the cliffs,
    show me your face,
    let me hear your voice,
    for your voice is pleasant
    and your face lovely."
15. Catch us the foxes,
    the little foxes,
    the destroyers of the vineyard;
    and our vineyard is budding.
16. My beloved is mine and I am his;
    he is a shepherd among the lilies.
17. "Before the morning breezes come
    and the shadows flee,
    come back, be like the gazelle, my love,

or the young fawn
on the mountains of sharing."

Third Poem

Chapter III

SHE

1. On my bed, at night, I sought
   the one my soul loves.
   I sought him, but did not find him.
2. I will get up then and roam the city;
   in the streets and through the squares
   I will look for the one my soul loves.
   I looked for him, but did not find him.

3. The watchmen met me,
   the ones who make the rounds of the city:
   "Have you seen the one my soul loves?"
4. Hardly had I left them,
   I found the one my soul loves.
   I grasped him and would not let him go,
   until I brought him
   to my mother's house,
   to the room of her who conceived me.

5. I put you under oath, daughters of Jerusalem,
   by the gazelles, by the wild does,
   do not rouse, do not waken Love
   before it so desires.

Fourth Poem

CHORUS

6. What is this coming up from the desert
    like a column of smoke,
    mist of myrrh and incense,
    of every exotic dust?

7. It is Solomon's litter:
    sixty heroes surround it,
    the elite of Israel's heroes,

8. all skilled with the sword,
    veterans of combat,
    each with a sword at his side
    ready for alarms in the night.

9. King Solomon made for himself
    a palanquin of wood from Lebanon.

10. He made its columns of silver,
    the canopy of gold,
    the seat of purple;
    the interior was lovingly worked on
    by the daughters of Jerusalem.

11. Daughters of Zion, come and gaze
    at King Solomon with the diadem
    with which his mother crowned him
    on his wedding day,
    on the day of his heart's delight.

Fifth Poem

Chapter IV

HE

1. How beautiful you are, my love,
    how beautiful you are!
    Your eyes are doves
    behind your veil.
    Your hair, like a flock of goats
    streaming down Mount Gilead.
2. Your teeth, a flock of ewes to be shorn
    coming up from the washing;
    each one has its twin,
    not one alone among them.
3. Your lips, a scarlet thread,
    and your voice, pleasant.
    Your cheeks, slices of pomegranate
    behind your veil.
4. Your neck is like the tower of David,
    built in courses;
    a thousand shields are hung on it,
    all the bucklers of heroes.
5. Your two breasts, two fawns,
    twins of a gazelle, feeding among the lilies.

6. Before the morning breezes come,
    and the shadows flee,
    I shall go away to the mountain of myrrh,
    to the hill of incense.

7. You are all beautiful, my love,
    without blemish of any kind.

8. Come[1] from Lebanon, my bride to be,
   come[1]from Lebanon, make your entree,
   hurry from the peaks of Amana,
   the peaks of Senir and Hermon,
   den of lions,
   mountain of leopards.

9. You drive me out of my mind,
   my sister, my promised bride,
   you drive me out of my mind
   with a single one of your glances,
   with just one bead of your necklace.

10. What charms your caresses bring,
    my sister, my promised bride;
    your caresses, how delightful they are,
    even more than wine,
    and the aroma of your perfumes,
    even more than all spices!

11. Your lips, my promised bride,
    distil nectar;
    honey and milk are under your tongue,
    and the aroma of your clothes
    is like the aroma of Lebanon.

12. She is a garden enclosed,
    my sister, my promised bride,
    a garden[2] enclosed,
    a fountain sealed.

13. Your shoots are an orchard of pomegranates
    with choicest fruits, henna with nard,

---

[1] "Come," *'ĕtî*, versions; *'ittî*, "with me," MT.

[2] "Garden," *gan*, Hebrew mss. and versions; *gal*, "spring," MT.

14. nard and saffron,
    calamus and cinnamon
    with every incense-bearing tree,
    myrrh and aloes
    with the finest of spices;
15. a fountain of the gardens,
    a well of living waters
    flowing down from Lebanon.

SHE

16. Wake up, north wind,
    hurry up, south wind.
    Make my garden breathe
    and so spread its aroma!
    May my beloved enter his garden
    and taste its choicest fruits!

Chapter V

HE

1. I come into my garden,
   my sister, my promised bride;
   I gather my myrrh and balm;
   I eat my honeycomb with my honey;
   I drink my wine with my milk.

CHORUS

Eat my friends,
drink, drink well, dear ones.

Sixth Poem

SHE

2. I sleep, but my heart is awake.
   I hear my beloved knocking:
   "Open to me, my sister, my love,
   my dove, my perfect one,
   for my head is wet with dew,
   my hair with the dampness of night."

3. I have taken off my clothes;
   should I put them on again?
   I have washed my feet,
   should I soil them again?

4. My beloved thrust his hand through the slot,
   and for him my innermost being quivered.

5. For my part, I got up to open to my beloved
   and my hands exuded myrrh;
   my fingers, myrrh dripping
   on the handle of the bolt.

6. I opened to my beloved,
   but my beloved, turning his back, had disappeared.
   Beside myself, I go out to follow him;
   I look for him, but do not find him;
   I call him, but he does not answer.

7. The watchmen met me,
   the ones who make the rounds of the city.
   They beat me, they bruised me,
   they took away my shawl,
   they who watch the walls.

8. I put you under oath, daughters of Jerusalem,

if you find my beloved,
what must you tell him?
that I am love-sick.

Seventh Poem

CHORUS

9. What does your beloved have more than others,[1]
   O most beautiful of women?
   What does your beloved have more than others,[1]
   that you put us under such an oath?

SHE

10. My beloved is clear ochre;
    he would stand out among ten thousand.
11. His head is of gold, pure gold;
    his locks are palm branches,
    black as the raven.
12. His eyes are doves
    beside the water-courses,
    bathing in milk,
    at rest on a pool.
13. His cheeks, beds of spices,
    clusters delightfully scented.
    His lips, lilies;
    they distill dripping myrrh.
14. His hands, golden sockets
    studded with stones from Tarshish.

---

[1] Literally: "more than a beloved."

His belly, a block of ivory
covered with lapis lazuli.
15.   His legs, columns of alabaster,
set on pedestals of pure gold.
His appearance is that of Lebanon,
as choice as the cedars.
16.   His mouth is sweetness itself,
and his whole being is completely charming.
Such is my beloved, such is my loved one,
daughters of Jerusalem.

Chapter VI

CHORUS

1.   Which way then has your beloved gone,
O most beautiful of women?
Which way then has your beloved turned,
that we may help you look for him?

SHE

2.   My beloved has gone down to his garden,
to the bed of spices,
to be a shepherd in the gardens
and to gather lilies.
3.   I am my beloved's and my beloved is mine,
he is a shepherd among the lilies.

Eighth Poem

HE

4. You are beautiful as Tirzah, my love,
   enchanting as Jerusalem, formidable as armies.
5. Turn your eyes away from me,
   for they entrance me.
   Your hair is a flock of goats
   streaming down Gilead.
6. Your teeth a flock of ewes
   coming up from the washing;
   each one has its twin
   and not one alone among them.
7. Your cheeks, slices of pomegranate
   behind your veil.

8. There are sixty queens,
   and eighty concubines,
   and young girls without number.
9. My dove, my perfect one, stands out;
   she is the one for her mother;
   the favorite of her who bore her.
   The young girls saw and praised her;
   queens and concubines extolled her.
10. "Who is this who comes up as the dawn,
    fair as the moon,
    radiant as the sun,
    formidable as armies?"

Ninth Poem

SHE

11. To the walnut garden I went down
     to see the young sprouts in the wadi,
     to see if the vines are budding,
     if the pomegranates are in flower.
12. I knew not my heart,
     it made of me the chariots of Ammi-nadib.

Chapter VII

CHORUS

1. Come back, come back, O Shulamite,
    come back, come back that we may gaze at you!

HE

What are you looking at in the Shulamite
as in a dance of two camps?

2. How beautiful are your feet in sandals,
    O prince's daughter!
    The curves of your thighs are like necklaces,
    work of an artist's hand.
3. Your lap, a rounded cup
    where blended wine is never lacking!
    Your belly, a heap of wheat
    set about with lilies.
4. Your two breasts are like two fawns,
    twins of a gazelle.

5. Your neck is like a tower of ivory.
   Your eyes are like the pools of Heshbon,
   by the gate of Bath-Rabbim.
   Your nose is like the tower of Lebanon,
   a sentinel facing Damascus.
6. On you, your head is like Carmel,
   and the locks of your head are like purple;
   a king is bound in these tresses.
7. How beautiful you are, how delightful you are,
   love, daughter of[1] delights!

8. Your stature here is like the palm-tree;
   your breasts are its clusters.
9. I said, "I will climb the palm-tree;
   I will grasp its clusters.
   Let your breasts be like the clusters of grapes;
   the aroma of your breath, like that of apples;
10. your mouth like a delicious wine!"

SHE

It goes straight to my beloved;
it flows on the lips of sleepers.
11. I belong to my beloved
    and his desire is for me.

Tenth Poem

12. Come, my beloved,
    let us go out to the country.
    We will pass the night in the villages.

---

[1] *Bat ta 'ănûgîm*, versions; "in the delights," MT.

13. In the morning we will go in the vineyards;
     we will see if the vines are budding,
     if the bud is opening,
     if the pomegranates are in flower.
     There, I will give you my caresses.
14. The mandrakes give off their aroma;
     the best fruits are at our doors;
     the new as well as the old,
     I have set them aside for you, my beloved.

Chapter VIII

SHE

1. Oh that you were my brother,
    nursed at my mother's breast!
    Meeting you outside, I could kiss you
    without people scorning me.
2. I would lead you, I would bring you
    into my mother's house:
    you would teach me;
    I would make you drink spiced wine,
    juice of my pomegranate.

3. His left arm is under my head
    and his right embraces me.
4. I put you under oath, daughters of Jerusalem,
    do not rouse, do not awaken Love
    before it so desires.

Epilogue

CHORUS

5. Who is this coming up from the desert,
    leaning on her beloved?

SHE

Under the apple tree I awaken you,
there where your mother conceived you,
there where she who bore you conceived you.

6. Put me as a seal on your heart,
    as a seal on your arm.

For Love is strong as death;
jealousy, unyielding as Sheol;
its flashes are like flashes of fire,
a flame of YHWH.

7. Mighty waters cannot
    quench Love.
    Floods will not submerge it.
    If one gave for Love
    all the possessions of his house,
    he certainly would be scorned.

Additions

CHORUS

8. Our sister is little,
    and she has no breasts.

What will we do for our sister
on the day she shall be spoken for?

9. If she is a wall,
    we will build on her
    parapets of silver;
    if she is a door,
    we will fasten on her
    planks of cedar.

SHE

10. I am a wall
     and my breasts are its towers;
     therefore, I am in his eyes
     as one who has found peace.

✳

11. Solomon had a vineyard at Baal Hamon.
     He entrusted it to overseers;
     each one will be made to pay for his fruit
     a thousand pieces of silver.

SHE

12. My own vineyard is before me;
     the thousand is yours, Solomon,
     and two hundred for the guardians of the fruit.

✳

HE

13. You who dwell in the gardens,
    companions give ear to your voice;
    make me hear.

SHE

14. Flee, my beloved,
    and be like the gazelle
    or the young fawn
    on the mountains of spices.

Chapter One

STRUCTURE AND DIVISIONS

*T*he traditional division of the Song of Songs into eight chapters of varying length seems to have had a mainly utilitarian purpose. Two manuscripts of the Septuagint, Alexandrinus and Sinaiticus, would suggest some changes in speakers; these indications are more developed in Codex Sinaiticus.[1] In the twelfth century Abbé Rupert distinguished four parts, marked off by the awakening refrain: "I put you under oath, daughters of Jerusalem, by the gazelles, by the wild does, do not rouse, do not awaken Love before it so desires" (2:7; 3:5; 8:4).[2] Modern critics generally consider the Song of Songs to be an anthology of poems of greater or less length, brought together into a continuous work by one or more redactors. To separate these poems, one must take note not only of refrains in the strict sense of the word, but also of numerous repetitions and *mots crochets*. However, agreement on the number of poems is still not yet in sight. The following summary will let you judge for yourself.

A. Robert (1963) singled out five poems; J. C. Exum (1973), six; D. Buzy (1940) and D. Lys (1968), seven; J. Angénieux (1965), eight; J. M. Reese (1983), ten; M. D. Goulder (1986), fourteen; I. Bettan (1950), eighteen; N. Schmidt (1911), nineteen; K. Budde (1898), twenty-three; O. Eissfeldt (1965), twenty-five; M. Haller (1940), twenty-six; R. Gordis (1954), twenty-eight; E. Würhtwein (1967), O. Loretz (1966) and J. B. White (1978), thirty; M. Falk (1982), thirty-one; J. Segert (1956) and G. Gerleman (1965), thirty-two; L. Krinetzki (1964), fifty-two.[3] M. Pope mentions a fifteenth-century German paraphrase of the Song which divided the book into forty-four parts.[4] He also refers to a study of R. Kessler (1957) which divided the book into four parts of almost equal length: 1:2 to 2:17 (thirty-three verses); 3:1 to 5:1 (twenty-eight verses); 5:2 to 7:1 (twenty-eight verses); 7:2 to 8:14 (twenty-seven verses).[5] Finally, M. Pope gives up on proposing a logical division.

However, the presence of a great number of repetitions throughout the whole work would indicate instead a certain literary unity.[6] For example, the heroine of the Song often addresses the "daughters of Jerusalem." She begins to do this after the first two strophes (1:5) and continues in the three "awakening" refrains (2:7; 3:5; 8:4), and elsewhere as well: 3:11 (here, "daughters of Zion"); 5:8 and 16 (followed by the reply of the daughters in 6:1). They are again probably the ones who begin to speak in 6:10 and 7:1 in a way that reminds us of a chorus. In the same way the compliment "O most beautiful of women" (1:8) is repeated by the daughters in 5:9 and 6:1. The function of these interventions, often attributed to a chorus, is open to discussion, but, whatever it is, they do indicate each time a pause in the progress of the Song.

It is agreed that 2:6–7 serves as a conclusion to the first long poem: "His left hand is under my head and his right embraces me. I put you under oath, daughters of Jerusalem, etc." The same should be true of 8:3–4: "His left hand is under my head and his right embraces me. I put you under oath, daughters of Jerusalem, do not rouse, do not awaken Love before it so desires." Only the line "by the gazelles, by the wild does" is missing.

The refrain of mutual belonging: "My beloved is mine and I am his; he is a shepherd among the lilies" (2:16) occurs first near the end of a poem which concludes in 2:17: "Come back, be like the gazelle, my love, or the young fawn on the mountains of sharing." This comes just before the account of the first quest (3:1–5). The last verse of the Song (8:14) repeats part of this phrase:

"Flee, my beloved, and be like the gazelle or the young fawn on the mountains of spices." In 6:3 the refrain of mutual belonging can also be used to conclude a poem. It is partially repeated in 7:11 in an inverted form: "I belong to my beloved and his desire is for me." Once again, we can pick out the end of a poem from the invitation that follows: "Come, my beloved" (7:12).

In 3:6 the description of the wedding procession of Solomon is introduced by the question: "What is this coming up from the desert like a column of smoke?" In 8:5 the similar question, "Who is this coming up from the desert, leaning on her beloved?" introduces the announcement of the definitive consummation of love, of a union sealed forever. These two questions mark in each case the beginning of a poem.

Starting from these literary considerations, we can determine the limits of a certain number of poems and at the same time avoid dividing them up in an arbitrary way; however, we must keep in mind all the repetitions, so characteristic of the Song of Songs. Modern criticism has had a field day in altering the received text to make it conform more to our western logic. But the prehistory of the Song will always be beyond our reach. Omitting verses or moving them around will remain weak and uncontrollable hypotheses. Therefore, we will attempt here to find ways to understand better the traditional received text, along with its possible complements—in other words, the text in its entirety.

*

*   *

The title of the Song of Songs (1:1), with the mention of Solomon, is followed by a prologue made up of two symmetrical strophes of five stichs each (vv. 2–3 and v. 4), both ending with the same verb "they *love* you." Then the first poem begins (1:5–2:7); it contains the only real dialogue between the two young people. The young woman begins and ends the dialogue. Her first words (1:5–7) are interrupted by the chorus of the young women of Jerusalem, already addressed in verse 5. Immediately after, the young man praises his "loved one"; she replies, calling him four times her "beloved"; she also refers to him as "king," as she had already done in the prelude in verse 4. The expression "the vineyards of En Gedi," that is to say, "the eye of the goat," in verse 14 links together verse 6 (the vineyards), verse 8 (the goats) and verse 15 (the eyes).

In the second poem (2:8–17), it is the young woman who speaks; she mentions a call from her beloved in verses 10 to 14. The expression "my beloved" appears at the beginning (vv. 8, 9, 10) and at the end (vv. 16, 17) of the poem. Likewise, the words "gazelle" and "young fawn" (literally, "fawn of the does") which are found in the refrain of 2:7 reappear at the end of the poem in 2:17.

The third poem (3:1–5) describes the first nocturnal search by the young woman for "the one my soul loves." This phrase is repeated four times by her in these verses; the same is true of the verb "seek." The meeting actually takes place; but it is not yet the moment "to awaken Love." A. Robert thought that this was a way of poetically calling to mind the relationship of YAHWEH and his spouse, Israel.[7] As I will show eventually, I hope, it is a question rather of the relationship between the messianic Solomon and the daughter of Zion. If this is so, the following poem (3:6–11) occurs in its rightful place, for it describes the wedding procession of King Solomon. He is named three times in this fourth poem, in which he is the central figure, idealized as in the book of Chronicles (1 Chron. 28 and 29; 2 Chron. 9). We will return to this later.

This fourth poem is connected by a series of *mots crochets* to the preceding poem: my mother/his mother (3:4 and 11); the nights (3:1 and 8); the presence of guards who make the rounds and surround the litter (Hebrew *sbyb, sbbym;* 3:3 and 7). The daughters of Jerusalem are again mentioned and addressed as the "daughters of Zion" (a phrase that occurs just this once in the Song).

In the fifth poem (4:1–5:1), the phrase "my sister, my promised bride" (4:9,10,12; 5:1) or simply "my promised bride" (4:11) makes clear the unity of the poem and can be understood perfectly after the preceding poem which brought to mind the nuptial procession and wedding of Solomon. Solomon for the first time speaks the praise of his well-beloved in a literary genre similar to the *wasf* of Arab love poems. This fifth poem can be easily subdivided, making use of the inclusions interspersed by the poet: "How beautiful you are, my love" (4:1 and 7), "Lebanon" (4:8 and 11), "the garden" (4:12,15 and 5:1). The young woman intervenes only at the end (4:16) to invite her beloved to enter her garden, which he immediately does. The final words, "Eat, my friends, drink, drink well, dear ones" (5:1f-g), can be addressed to the two lovers and mark a major interlude in the booklet; we are as a matter of fact in the middle of the Song of Songs.[8]

The sixth poem (5:2–8) takes up in a more dramatic fashion the theme of the nocturnal search, already developed in the third poem. This time the search is in vain; it is a missed rendezvous. Beaten, bruised, stripped of her shawl by the guards, the young woman calls on the daughters of Jerusalem to intervene with her beloved; as long as he is absent, she is "love-sick."[9] The poem ends therefore like the first poem (2:5), where the young woman already admits being love-sick. The expression "my sister, my love" (5:2) links this poem with the preceding one. The *mot crochet* "my beloved" is repeated six times in this sixth poem and forms an inclusion at the beginning (5:2) and end (5:8).

This same *mot crochet* "my beloved" recurs several times at the beginning (5:9–10) and end (5:16 and 6:1–3) of the seventh poem. This poem (5:9 to 6:3) infers that the search for the beloved continues. In his absence, the young woman praises him in a curious and unaccustomed manner (5:10–16), which at the end leads to a question by the daughters of Jerusalem; they offer to help the young woman who affirms once more that she belongs to the one she loves (6:3 repeats the refrain of 2:16). The seventh poem ends then in the same way the second one does.

The eighth poem begins like the fifth poem: "You are beautiful" (6:4), "How beautiful you are!" (4:1). This second praise—or *wasf*—of the young girl by her beloved begins abruptly then. Here again, the presence of the young man is not indicated before we hear the words that he addresses to his well-beloved. He had been presented merely as a "shepherd" at the end of the previous poem, whereas 3:11 (the end of the fourth poem) presented him as King Solomon. The beginning and end of this eighth poem are clearly indicated by the inclusion: "beautiful as . . . formidable as armies."

The ninth poem (6:11 to 7:11) is more complex. The third praise—or *wasf*—of the young woman, spoken by the young man (7:2ff.), begins with the feet of the dancer, as it should, following the last words of verse 1 which speak of this dance. The gaze begins below and moves up, the very opposite of the first *wasf* (4:1ff.). The word *nādîb*, "prince" forms a link between 6:12 ("the chariots of Ammi-*nādîb*") and 7:2 ("prince's daughter"). The poem begins with the words of the young woman in 6:11–12, before the chorus breaks in, addressing her as the Shulamite. This characteristic name, derived from *šālôm*, also brings to mind the name of Solomon. The importance of this passage for the correct interpretation of the Song of Songs is obvious. At the end of the ninth poem the young woman interrupts her beloved to complete his phrase, "Your mouth like a delicious wine!" by adding: "It goes straight to my beloved; it flows on the lips of sleepers." It finishes off by repeating once more the refrain of mutual belonging with which the second and seventh poems ended; however, the refrain is modified: "I belong to my beloved and his desire is for me."

The tenth poem (7:12–8:4) begins in a way that resembles the beginning of the preceding poem. The sentence "Let us go see if the vines are budding, if the pomegranates are in flower" (6:11) is repeated in 7:13. The invitation "Come" (7:12) indicates that the end of the poem is near. The two young people will go together into the gardens, as soon as it is morning. For now then, it is still night time, the same as in the third and sixth poems on the "nocturnal search." We must also take note of the verbs in the first person plural in verses 12 and 14 just as in the first poem (1:16–17). The tenth poem ends with a refrain (8:3–4) precisely like that at the end of the first poem (2:6–7). Once more the young woman reminds the daughters of Jerusalem that they must not awaken Love before it so desires. The first poem had already spoken in 1:13 of the sleep of the young man: "He passes the night between my breasts." We will see later on the importance to be given to this "sleep."

The epilogue of the Song (8:5–7) begins with a question posed by the chorus of young women: "Who is this coming up from the desert, leaning on her beloved?" This question recalls the one which introduced the fourth poem (3:6): "What is this coming up from the desert . . . ?" The answer is given by the young woman as she addresses her beloved: "Under the apple tree I awaken you. . . . " The mention of the apple tree recalls the reference to apples in 2:3. Above all, the young woman announces that the moment of *awakening* has at last arrived for the one she loves. But he must definitively seal their *love*. This essential word is repeated three times in 8:6–7, exactly as at the end of the first poem (2:4–5 and 7). This symmetry is remarkable and constitutes a clearly-intended inclusion. On the other hand, the repetitions just mentioned converge to give to the Song a certain literary unity from beginning to end, even before any discussion of its interpretation. It is true that the verses which conclude the epilogue (8:6–7) are written in a didactic and aphoristic style, very different from the lyrical style in the preceding parts. But does the poet not wish to draw out here the lesson of the ten poems? It will be necessary to try to understand this conclusion well and to determine precisely what Love is being spoken of here. But it would be a mistake to neglect the literary affinities between 8:1– 4 and 8:5–7: the same interrogative pronoun in 8:1 and 5 (*mî*, "who?"); same verb "to give" in 8:1 (literally: "Who will give you to me as a brother?") and 8:7; same verb "to scorn" in 8:1 and 7; same mention of the "mother" in 8:1–2 and 5; of the "house" in 8:2 and 7; of the preposition "under" in 8:3 and 5. One suspects here the hand of the same author in spite of the difference in style.

It is a different matter in regard to the end of chapter 8. Most critics consider verses 8 to 14 as one or several additions, attached later to the initial booklet. We must ask then why they were added and investigate whether or not they also have a certain unity. Without wishing to clear up all the problems presented by these last verses, it is not out of place to make some observations. We cannot abstract from these verses in the general interpretation of the Song, for they represent a certain "reading," if not a "re-reading," of the whole work at the oldest level of Jewish exegesis. Replying to the remarks of the chorus, the young woman in verse 10 continues with the same metaphor of the fortified city, with a wall, parapets, a door and . . . towers.[10] We think immediately of *Yĕrûšālem*, here identified with the Shulamite: "I am in *his* eyes (those of 'Solomon,' her beloved) as one who has found peace, *šālôm*." This Jerusalem can only be the holy city restored by Nehemiah; he rebuilt the walls and fixed the doors to the gates (Neh. 6:1; cf. Ez. 38:11). The canticle of Tobit (13:12) speaks in connection with Jerusalem of walls, towers and houses with the verb "build" as in Song 8:9. In Isaiah 60:18 there is again mention of walls and gates of Zion; the same is true of Isaiah 54:12, etc. It should be noted also that the only other use of the verb *dbr*, "to speak," in the *pual* (passive) is in a specific reference to Jerusalem in Psalm 87:3: "Glorious things are spoken of you." Therefore, Song 8:8–10 seems here to identify in a symbolic way the heroine of the Song with the daughter of Zion, Jerusalem.

In verses 11–12 the name of Solomon immediately follows the word *šālôm*, "peace" with which verse 10 ends. This definitely refers to the king who brings peace to Jerusalem, which is perhaps referred to here under the enigmatic place name of Baal Hamon which is otherwise unknown in either Palestine or Transjordan. The word *hāmôn* means a noisy crowd and is applied to Jerusalem in several texts.[11] The symbols of the "vineyard" and "garden" remind us of the images in 1:6–8 of the first poem, with the same Aramaic verb *ntr*, "to guard." It is tempting to compare the numbers of the thousand pieces of silver (v. 11; cf. Gen. 20:16) and of the thousand women—wives (three hundred) and concubines (seven hundred)—of which 1 Kings 11:3 speaks in regard to Solomon. It seems that it is the young woman who addresses Solomon in verse 12; she tells him that her vineyard, the vineyard of the daughter of Zion, is "before her," that is to say, at her complete disposal (for the meaning intended, cf. 2 Chron. 14:6). She therefore repeats what she had already said to "the daughters of Jerusalem" in telling them that she has found peace; she is from now on free to act as she wishes. The time is over when her "brothers" could reproach her for not guarding the vineyard (1:6).

This passage (see p. 118) has not yet been clarified, even though important studies have been done and learned hypotheses developed.[12] It is of interest to note in the poetical praise of Simon Maccabaeus (1 Macc. 14:8–12) a certain number of contacts: the earth is cultivated in peace and the trees yield their fruit; the cities are provided with fortifications (1 Macc. 13:33 mentions towers, walls, gates with bars); the country is at peace and each one sits under his own vine.

Verses 13–14 of this final chapter recall 2:8,12,14 and 17 of the second poem. In verse 14, the last verse of the Song of Songs, "my beloved" is the thirty-third mention of *dôd*, "the beloved," which is perhaps intentional (see p. 119). The beloved begs his well-beloved to tell him to flee; she had already asked him to leave with her (7:12). We have then a definitive departure here at the end of the booklet. . . .

*

*   *

---

[1]   Cf. A. RAHLFS, *Septuaginta*, II, 1935, pp. 270–71. Note *pros ton nymphion christon* in 1:7, a heading which presupposes a Christian messianic interpretation.

[2]   MIGNE, *Patrologia Latina*, vol. 168, col. 839.

[3]   See the extensive bibliography published in M. H. POPE, *Song of Songs*, pp. 252–58 and the bibliographies in the other commentaries on the Song of Songs. G. KRINETZKI, *Hoheslied* (Die Neue Echter Bibel, Würzburg, 1980) maintains the division into fifty-two poems which he had already proposed in his 1964 commentary. F. LANDY, *Paradoxes of Paradise: Identity and Difference in the Song of Songs* (The Almond Press, Sheffield, 1983), has a more recent extensive bibliography, pp. 363–86.

[4]   POPE, p. 40. See the review of POPE by R. TOURNAY, *RB* 86 (1979), pp. 137–40.

[5]   POPE, p. 49.

[6]   Cf. R. E. MURPHY, "The Unity of the Song of Songs," *VT* 29 (1979), pp. 137–40 and "Cant 2:8–17—A Unified Poem?" in *Mélanges bibliques et orientaux en l'honneur de M. Mathias Delcor* (AOAT 215, 1985), pp. 305–10. Likewise, W. H.

SHEA, "The Chiastic Structure of the Song of Songs," *ZAW* 92 (1980), pp. 378–96; he distinguishes six sections: 1:2–2:2 and 8:6–14; 2:3–17 and 7:11–8:5; 3:1–4:16 and 5:1–7:10. We would have then a chiastic structure: A : B : C :: C' : B' : A'. See also E. C. WEBSTER, "Pattern in the Song of Songs," *JSOT* 22 (1982), 73–93 for a different chiastic pattern. F. LANDY, *Paradoxes of Paradise* . . . , discusses the unity of the Song on pp. 33–39 and throughout his whole book: " . . . exploration of the unity of the Song will be coterminous with this work . . . " (p. 39).

7   A. ROBERT (*Le Cantique des Cantiques*, Études Bibliques, Paris, 1963) joined 3:1–5 to 2:8–17 to form a single poem, the second. He likewise joined 4:1–5 to 3:6–11 to form a single poem, the third. The fourth poem went, according to him, from 5:2 to 6:3; and the fifth, from 6:4 to 8:5a. I followed A. Robert in *Le Cantique des Cantiques, Commentaire abrégé* (Lire la Bible 9, Le Cerf, Paris, 1967). Here I propose a new division into ten poems. I diverge from A. Robert on several important points, especially on the meaning of the "awakening" of the young man who represents, in my view, the new Solomon of the messianic era.

8   The *Parva Massora* which counted 117 verses in the Song noted that the mid-point of the booklet was at 4:14 *nrd wkrkm*.

9   This translation was suggested to me by Pierre Grelot.

10   According to 2 Chron. 14:6 King Asa proposed to Judah that the fortress cities of Judah be restored with walls, towers, gates, and bars. The theme of the woman-city is found throughout the Ancient East (see below, p. 48).

11   Is. 32:14; Ps. 42:5; Joel 4:14; cf. Lam. 1:1. See G. GERLEMAN, "Die lärmende Menge" in *Wort und Geschichte—Festschrift K. Elliger* (AOAT 18, 1973), pp. 71–75.

[12] In particular those of A. ROBERT, *op. cit.*, pp. 314–26 and earlier *RB* 55 (1948), pp. 161–83. He identified the vineyard with all of Palestine. In regard to the vineyards of David and of Solomon, cf. 1 Chron. 27:27 and Ecclesiastes 2:4. See most recently F. LANDY, "Beauty and the Enigma: An Inquiry into Some Interrelated Episodes of the Song of Songs," *JSOT* 17 (1980), pp. 71–85 and *Paradoxes of Paradise* . . . , pp. 152–69.

Chapter Two

The Celebration of Solomon's Love Affairs

*T*he very beginning of the Song of Songs would be the place
where we would expect to find some clues to the meaning of
this love poem. A thorough analysis of these first verses is called
for then before any other investigation. This alone will allow us
to find out what should be the most adequate interpretation of
this booklet. It is in the *prologue* that the appropriate key should
be found for introducing us into the authentic meaning of this en-
tire poetic work.

Here is the translation of the prologue (verses 2–4):

2. Let him kiss me with the kisses of his mouth,
    for more delicious than wine are your caresses.
3. As for fragrance, your perfumes are a delight;
    a delicate perfume is your NAME;
    this is why the maidens *love you*.
4. Draw me after you, let us run;
    the King shows me to his room.
    Let us rejoice, let us make merry because of you;
    we will celebrate your caresses more than wine;
    how rightly do they *love you*.

These two symmetrical strophes (5 + 5 stichs) end with the
same form of the same verb "to love"; they repeat the same phrase
"your caresses more than wine." It is the young woman who
speaks right from the beginning and moreover it is she who will
speak most often in the rest of the Song. Already then there is a

major difference from the Egyptian love songs, where the young man has the long discourses; otherwise, the Egyptian love songs are very similar to the Song.[1]

If the young woman wishes to be kissed passionately,[2] the reason would be that she already knows perfectly the one whom she calls "my beloved" and whose NAME (*šēm*), belonging to him alone, says everything about him. She compares it to a delicate perfume.[3] A succession of paronomasias, alliterations and assonances draws attention to the NAME of Solomon.[4] If the first two words of verse 2, derived from the same root *nšq*, resemble the sound of kissing, the cumulative effect of the "shushing" sound of the sibilant *šin* together with the liquid consonants (*lamed*, *mem*, *nun*, *reš*) brings to mind *šĕlōmōh*, Solomon. The words *šēm*, name, and *šemen*, oil or perfume (twice) form an expressive play on words which is also found in Ecclesiastes 7:1. The oil could allude to the anointing of the messiah king, the anointed: Solomon was so anointed (1 Kgs. 1:34–39). God anoints the messiah with oil of gladness (Ps. 45:8); this verse of the psalm begins with *'al-kēn*, "this is why, therefore," a phrase found in the Song only at the end of verse 3 of the prologue: "this is why the maidens love you." It should be noted that Psalm 45, which celebrates the marriage of the messiah king and his spouse, resembles the Song in many ways, so much so that the two texts should be interpreted in a similar way.[5]

The name *šĕlōmōh*, Solomon,[6] is derived from *šālôm*, "peace," as is also the name of his brother *'Abšālôm*, Absalom. The author of 1 Chronicles 22:9 is very much aware of this: "Look—God said to David—a son will be born to you. He will be a man of peace and I will give him rest from his enemies on every side; for Solomon is to be his name (*šemô*), and in his days I shall give Israel peace (*šālôm*) and tranquility." We have already noted the bringing together of *šālôm* and *šĕlōmōh* in Song 8:10–11. Psalm 72, attributed to Solomon in the title, may be mentioned as a similar example: this psalm announces the coming of peace in verses 3 and 7 and proclaims in verse 17 that the NAME of this "son of a king" (verse 1: an allusion to Solomon, son of David) will be blessed (Septuagint; M.T. omits this word) forever. Isaiah (9:2–5) predicts the coming of the Prince of peace in exultation and joy. This oracle is echoed in Micah 5, where the one who is to rule Israel will be PEACE (verse 4). The same idea is present in Zechariah 9:9–10: "Rejoice (*gyly*, the same verb as in Song 1:4b) heart and soul, daughter of Zion! Shout for joy, daughter of Jerusalem! Look, *your king* is approaching. . . . He proclaims *peace* to the nations." Finally, Sirach 47:16, speaking of Solomon, presents once again, at the beginning of the second century B.C.E., the equation *šĕlōmōh/šālôm:* "Your NAME reached the distant islands and you were loved for *your peace.*"

Other examples of paronomasia[7] should be noted in the prologue of the Song (in addition to *šēm, šĕlōmōh, šemen*): namely, *moškēnî* (from the verb *mšk*), "draw me"; *melek,* "king"; *mēyšarîm,* "rightly" (an adverb meaning "justly, honestly"); *'ălāmôt,* "the young women." All these combinations of the "shushing" sound of *šin* with the liquid consonants recall the resonances of the NAME *šĕlōmōh.*

It is also possible that the word *dodêkā,* "your caresses" (twice) is to bring to mind the special name of Solomon, *yĕdîdyâ,* "beloved of YHWH" (2 Sam. 12:25). But a comparison should also be made with the word *dôd,* "beloved," which is used so often in the Song and which is spelled in Hebrew like the name of David, the father of Solomon. There will be a special study on this later (pp. 112ff).

The verbs *gyl* and *śmḥ,* "rejoice, make merry," placed side by side in verse 4, belong to the vocabulary of Covenant, as D. Lys has correctly noted.[8] Here this fact, along with the paronomasias already referred to, leads us toward a messianic perspective in which Solomon designates the future Messiah. The celebration of the love affairs of Solomon, announced in the prologue of the Song, has as its objective then the indefectible love of the daughter of Zion for the Solomon whom she awaits, but who is already present to her through his NAME, a substitute for his person. Far from being inserted into the Song, as some exegetes have claimed, the name of Solomon is essential here. Eliminating it would mean that understanding the Song would no longer be possible, since this would involve the ignoring of indications provided by the poet right from the opening verses through the play on the sound of words as well as through the choice of words. It is not YHWH the King that the daughter of Zion expects, as A. Robert and others have thought; it is the *new Solomon*, a king to whom she is engaged by virtue of the promises of the Covenant.[9] This is why she rejoices and makes merry with the daughters of Jerusalem at the moment when she is going to enter the chamber of the King. We may quote here the parallel reference in Psalm 45:15–16: "The king's daughter is led within to the king, with the maidens of her retinue. Her companions are brought to her; making merry and rejoicing, they enter the king's palace."

The central place provided for Solomon in the Song should not surprise us. It corresponds to the place he occupies in the book of Chronicles. The builder of the temple shares with David the essential role, according to this historian from the end of the fourth century B.C.E., for whom liturgy and worship constitute the principal activity of the people of YHWH and his ministers. The Chronicler carefully eliminates the shadows over the reign of Solomon mentioned in the book of Kings and idealizes the son of David, a prototype of the Messiah expected by Israel.

✳

✳   ✳

Immediately after the prologue, right from the beginning of

the first poem (1:5), the young woman speaks to her companions, the daughters of Jerusalem. This mention of the holy city, at this place in the Song, takes on great importance, inasmuch as it precedes by a few words, in the same verse, the mention of the pavilions of Solomon, in parallelism with the tents of Kedar.[10] The people of Kedar (cf. Gen. 25:13; Ps. 120:5) lived in Northern Arabia and controlled the incense routes in the Persian period (Is. 60:6–7). A. Lemaire has deciphered the name of a king of Kedar in an inscription on an incense altar discovered during excavations at Lachish.[11] It has been suggested then that the received Hebrew text should be corrected here from "Solomon" to "Salmah," namely, the country of Salomeans or Salmaites. The Targums in fact gave this name to the ancient Kenites from the Petra region, contemporaries of the people of Kedar.[12] The mention of Solomon in 1:5 would then be due to an editorial retouching; two other references to Solomon are found in 8:11–12, verses which could have been added by the final editor of the Song. This change to Solomon in 1:5 would make *seven* references to Solomon in the Song, just as there are seven to the daughters of Jerusalem, seven to Lebanon, etc.[13] By mentioning Solomon in 1:5, the editor in this way would have wanted to orient the reader from the very beginning toward a messianic interpretation of the Song, suggested, among other ways, by the description in 3:6–11 of the wedding procession of Solomon.[14]

The king of peace should rule over the city of peace, Jerusalem. Many texts suggest this traditional etymology of the name *yĕrûšālem*.[15] The end of the name, *šālem*, in actual fact designates the holy city in Psalm 76:3 which mentions Zion in parallelism with Salem. The same interpretation, moreover, is given in connection with the reference to Melchisedech, king of Salem (Gen. 14:18; Heb. 7:2). Psalm 122 multiplies the plays on words on Jerusalem, especially in verse 6 with the verbs *šā'al*, "to ask," and *šālâ*, "to be at rest"; the word *šālôm* comes up again three times, and also *šēm*, "the (divine) name" and *šām*, "there" (twice). According to the last verse of the book of Ezekiel (48:35), the name of Jerusalem in the future will be *YHWH-šāmmâ*, that is to say, "YHWH is there."[16] Psalm 76, referred to above, brings Jerusalem to mind through the adverb *šām*, "there"; several psalms repeat this paronomasia[17] which one is tempted to find in Song 8:5: the poet, in regard to the final awakening of the young man, repeats twice this adverb *šāmmâ*, "there." Incidentally, the paronomasia between *šēm*, the divine Name, and *šām*, "there," is found also in Deuteronomy 12:11,21; 14:23–24; 1 Kings 8:16,29; etc.

We will see later on (pp. 102–03) how the name given to the young woman, *šûlammît* (7:1) should be interpreted from this perspective. It is she who ends up by "finding peace," as she declares at the end of the book (8:10). She is truly the partner of Solomon, as her name indicates.[18] We should not be surprised if she is identified in 8:8–10 with the city of Jerusalem. The theme of the city as a woman is traditional in the whole ancient East. We need only cite the great Sumerian lamentation over the fall of the city of Ur, Abraham's native city according to Genesis 11:31. Jerusalem with the features of the daughter of Zion occupies the principal place in the second part of the book of Isaiah (49:14; 54:5) as well as in chapters 60, 62 and 66:7ff.[19] We could multiply the references by turning to texts which make use of the nuptial allegory in speaking of the Israelite nation. The verb *bānâ*, "to build" (Song 8:9; cf. 4:4) is used in speaking of a woman who has children; it is used in this way of Sarah (Gen. 16:2), Rachel (Gen. 30:3), Leah (Ruth 4:11; cf. Jer. 24:6; Deut. 25:9).

If the author of the prologue of the Song already implicitly suggests to us that the King Solomon whose love affairs he is going to celebrate is an ideal personage, a symbol of the Messiah expected by the daughter of Zion, it is natural to think that under the features of the heroine of the Song is hidden the holy City, dwelling of the Most High, city of peace, personification of a whole people, the community of Jews repatriated in the Persian period.[20] Nevertheless, we must not forget the historical starting point of the Song, namely, the marriage of Solomon to the daughter of Pharaoh, an Egyptian princess. Starting from this historical event, the poet, many centuries later, brings to mind the Solomon of the future.

We may add that the many geographical names contained in the Song, something unexpected in a simple love song, refer not only to Samaria (through Tirzah—6:4—whose name means Pleasure), but also to northern and southern Transjordan, as well as southern Syria (Damascus) and Lebanon, namely, an area corresponding to the territory in Solomon's empire before the schism of Jeroboam I, with perhaps an allusion to the treaty concluded between Solomon and King Hiram of Tyre (see pp. 125ff.).

*

*   *

---

[1] Cf. J. B. WHITE, *A Study of the Language of Love in the Song of Songs and Ancient Egyptian Poetry* (SBL DS, 38), Missoula, Montana, 1978, p. 174.

[2] "To be kissed passionately" seems to be the best translation of "embrassée à pleine bouche" which Tournay adopts here, as he mentions, from D. Lys, *Le plus beau chant de la création* (Lectio Divina 51), Paris, 1968, p. 62.

[3] Read *tamrûq* (MT *tûraq* is untranslatable); cf. Esther 2:3; 9:12; Prov. 20:30 is unclear. Pope merely transcribes *turaq* (pp. 291, 300).

[4] Cf. C. TRESMONTANT, *Esprit*, March 1963, p. 61; R. TOURNAY, *RB* 72 (1965), p. 430.

⁵ R. TOURNAY, "Les affinités du Ps XLV avec le Cantique des Cantiques et leur interprétation messianique," *Congress Volume Bonn 1962* (VTSup 9, 1963), pp. 168–212. Words and phrases are common to both: king, companion, maidens, virgins, beauty, myrrh, aloes, ivory, oil, gold, joy and exultation, "behind her/you," "to bring," "that I celebrate your name" (Ps. 45:18) and "let us celebrate" (Song 1:1). In regard to *zkr*, cf. W. SCHOTTROFF, *"Gedenken" im Alten Orient und im Alten Testament*, Neukirchen-Vluyn, 1964; this verb cannot be corrected to *škr*, "to make drunk" (LYS, p. 69). In regard to *'Elohîm* in Ps. 45:7, B. COUROYER presents the hypothesis that it could refer to a Ptolemy ("Dieu ou roi? Le vocatif dans le psaume XLV, 1–9," *RB* 78 [1971], p. 241).

⁶ Literally "his peace," "his integrity"; the masculine suffix would refer to David according to J. J. STAMM, "Der Name des Königs Salomo," *Beiträge für hebräischen und altorientalischen Namenkunde* (OBO 30, 1980), pp. 45–57. Cf. G. GERLEMAN, "Wurzel Salom," *ZAW* 85 (1973), pp. 1–14; C. WESTERMANN, "Der Frieden (Shalom) im Alten Testament," *Forschungen am A.T. Gesammelte Studien* 2 (1974), 196–229; H. WILDBERGER, *Jesaja* (BKAT 10/2, 1978), p. 1273 (on Is. 32:17–18); V. PETERCA, *L'immagine di Salomone nella Bibbia ebraica e graeca. Contributo allo studio del "Midrach"* (Pont. Univ. Gregor.), Rome, 1981, pp. 40–45.

⁷ Cf. V. PETERCA, *op. cit.*, p. 85; L. KRINETZKI, *Das Hohe Lied*, 1964, pp. 86–87.

⁸ LYS, p. 68. Cf. Ps. 9:3.

⁹ A. ROBERT had in mind the symbolic marriage of YHWH with Israel in the perspective of the marriage allegory developed by the prophets beginning with Hosea (cf. S. BITTER, *Die Ehe des Propheten Hosea*, Göttingen, 1975). But

he corrects himself on page 158: "Therefore, it is normal for the nation to crown, that is to say, to make king, the messianic sovereign." According to the New Testament, it is Jesus, the Messiah of Israel, who brings peace to people: "It is he who is our peace, he who from two peoples has made one" (Ephesians 2:14).

[10] This is a strange parallel. LYS tries to turn the difficulty around by seeing here a paraphrase to evoke the "magnificent curtains" (pp. 70–72). It should be noted that the word yry'wt, "pavilions," forms an alliteration with the verb tr'h, "pasture" (v. 7), as well as with r'y and r'ym (v. 8), "flock," "shepherds," and perhaps even with pr'h, Pharaoh (v. 9).

[11] Cf. *RB* 81 (1974), p. 63.

[12] Cf. Gen. 15:19; Num. 24:21; 1 Sam. 15:16; Judg. 4:17. See I. BEN ZVI, *Museon* 74 (1964), p. 154.

[13] Other objects named seven times in the Song: wine, myrrh, gazelle. Jerusalem is mentioned eight times, as also are lily, lotus and perfume (ryh).

[14] This passage is considered a later addition by M. Jastrow, J. T. Meek, O. Loretz, etc., because it cannot be considered a love song. But POPE (*op. cit.*, p. 433) regards such an omission as arbitrary, while at the same time he looks for a symbolic explanation of Solomon's name. LYS (*op. cit.*, pp. 154, 165) sees it as an early poem, composed for the marriage of Solomon to a foreign princess. But why would this be a quoted segment, earlier than the rest of the book?

[15] Is. 2:2–4; Mic. 4:1–4; Is. 11:6–9; 26:1–3; 32:17–18; 33:6–7; 52:7; 54:10ff; 65:25; Jer. 14:13,15,19; 23:16; 29:10–11; Ez. 13:16; 37:26; Hag. 2:9; Zech. 8:10,12,15–16,19,22; 9:9–10; Job 13:14–17; Bar. 4:20; 5:4; Judith 4:4; Ps. 147:12–14; etc. Cf. NORMAN W. PORTEOUS, *Living the*

Memory. Collected Essays, Oxford, 1967, chapter 7, "Jerusalem-Zion. The Growth of a Symbol," pp. 93–111; H.-J. KRAUS, *Theologie der Psalmen* (BKAT 15/3, 1960), pp. 100–01.

[16] In Ez. 40:1, the prophet says that God took him *over there*, on a very high mountain where the future city of Jerusalem will be built. We have here an inclusion with Ez. 48:35.

[17] In Ps. 66:6–7 "there" designates Jerusalem as F. CRÜSEMANN has well observed in *Studien zur Formgeschichte von Hymnus und Danklied in Israel*, 1969, p. 181. The same can be true in Ps. 14:5 (= 53:6); 36:13; 46:9; 48:7; 68:28; 87:4,6; 132:17; 137:3; Is. 33:21,24; 65:9,20; Jer. 7:12; 2 Sam. 6:2; 2 Chron. 7:16.

[18] Other possible allusions to the name of Solomon in Song would be the two names of numbers: *ššym*, "sixty" just before the mention of Solomon in 3:7 and in regard to the harem of Solomon in 6:8; and *šmnym*, "eighty," also in 6:8. We may also compare an oracle of the Assyrian king, Asarhaddon, which mentions sixty great gods standing round about him (ANET[3], p. 450).

[19] Cf. Baruch 4 and 5; Tob. 13:9–17; Rev. 21:1ff.

[20] Here I agree with the interpretation of G. NOLLI, *Cantico dei Cantici* (La Sacra Bibbia), Torino, 1968, pp. 44–45. He accepts a double meaning, one original and the other intended by the final redactor or editor. But he does not take into account the complementary aspect of these two meanings against the background of Jewish thinking in the Second Temple period in regard to the personality, at the same time historical and messianic, of King Solomon. C. HAURET ("Note d'Exégèse, Cantique des Cantiques, 1, 3: Introduxit me rex in cellaria sua," *RevScRel* 38 [1964], p. 70), at the end of his review of the book of Robert-Tournay, concluded: "The song of love, placed

on the lips of Solomon, would apply at the same time to
the son of David and to the future Messiah. Through the
union of Solomon and his spouse the scribe evokes the
union of the Messiah and his people. This double focus
especially justifies the extraordinary description of the
bride. It is worth noting that in the scribal period Solomon tended to become a type of the Messiah (cf. Chronicles and perhaps Ps. 72:1)." This is our opinion too.

Chapter Three

KING SOLOMON AND HIS EGYPTIAN SPOUSE

After having considered the *literary* starting point of the Song of Songs, we must now take up its *historical* starting point. It is none other than the marriage of Solomon to the daughter of the Egyptian Pharaoh. In fact, we read in 1 Kings 3:1, right at the beginning of the history of Solomon's reign, that "Solomon became the son-in-law of Pharaoh, king of Egypt; he married Pharaoh's daughter and brought her to the City of David until he could complete the building of his palace, the Temple of YHWH and the wall around Jerusalem." According to historians, the Pharaoh was Siamon or Psusennes II, kings of the twenty-first dynasty.[1] This marriage procured for Solomon the city of Gezer which the Pharaoh gave as dowry for his daughter, the wife of Solomon (1 Kgs. 9:16).[2] It is stated specifically in 1 Kings 7:8: "His own (Solomon's) living quarters were in a different court than the quarters set aside for a throne room; it was of the same construction. He also built a house for the daughter of Pharaoh whom he had married; it was similar to this throne room." A final detail is provided in 1 Kings 9:24: "It was only after Pharaoh's daughter had moved from the city of David up to the house that Solomon had built for her that he then built the Millo."[3]

The wife of Solomon was a pagan woman then. We can understand therefore the reflections of the second book of Chronicles (8:11) which repeats the text of 1 Kings 9:24, but adds to it a revealing commentary. The Levites of that time, at the end of the fourth century, were not in favor of marriages with pagan women, not to mention their preoccupation with the particular ritual impurities of women (the temple of Herod will have a court for women) and the prohibiting of foreigners from entering the sanctuary (Ez. 44:9). According to the Chronicler: "Solomon moved Pharaoh's daughter up from the city of David to the palace which he had built for her. For he said: 'My wife should not live in the house of David, king of Israel, for these buildings to which the ark of YHWH has come are sacred.'" The Targum on Chronicles goes further still: "Since these are sacred places, it is not permitted that a woman dwell there after the ark of YHWH has entered." The final section of the book of Nehemiah opposes mixed marriages between Jews and pagans and adds: "Was this not the way in which Solomon, king of Israel, sinned? Among many nations there was no king like him; he was loved by his God; God had made him king over all Israel. Even him the foreign women led into sinning" (Neh. 13:26; cf. earlier, Deut. 17:17).

Solomon was not the only one to marry an Egyptian princess. 1 Kings 11:18–20 describes how Hadad the Edomite took refuge in Egypt and married the sister of Pharaoh's wife, in other words, the sister of Tahpenes, "wife of the king," the Great Lady. His son Genubath was brought up in Pharaoh's palace. It was to Egypt too that Jeroboam fled; he lived near the Pharaoh Shishak until the death of Solomon (1 Kings 11:40; cf. 12:2). In addition, Solomon gathered around him Egyptian officials[4] and also developed commercial relations with Egypt as well as with Phoenicia and the kingdom of Saba. Egyptian writings as well as scribes must have come to Jerusalem where their wisdom literature, their tales, their love songs would be known. What would be more natural than to celebrate the marriage of Solomon and Pharaoh's daughter by looking to these love songs for inspiration? Gaston Maspéro had already shown as early as 1883 the resemblance between the Harris papyrus, the papyrus of Turin, and the Song of Songs.[5] Biblical scholars and Egyptologists have multiplied the references to works in this field of comparative literature.[6] It will suffice here to mention a few comparisons which show the intentions of the poet trying to give local Egyptian color to the Song, in order to call to mind the marriage of Solomon and Pharaoh's daughter.

Theodore of Mopsuestia (died 428) already saw in the Song a poem celebrating this marriage. He noted that Jewish women made fun of the Egyptian woman because of her dark complexion. Solomon, deeply hurt by this, retorted by singing his love for the Egyptian woman.[7] As is known, the Fifth Ecumenical Council condemned this interpretation *infanda Christianorum auribus* ("as offensive to Christian ears"). The mistake Theodore of Mopsuestia made was in limiting the interpretation to the historical Solomon without seeing in him the type of the Messiah expected by the daughter of Zion.

Certainly the first words of the young woman, "I am browned, but beautiful" (1:5), are very well understood on the lips of an Egyptian with dark skin, tanned by the African sun. Dom Calmet had already thought of this, but without mention of Egypt. To see in this darkness a symbol of the hardships undergone by the daughter of Zion, exiled and persecuted because of her infidelities, is not worth considering (this was A. Robert's explanation). Still more conjectural would be an allusion to the cult of black virgins and certain divinities, as M. H. Pope proposes.[8] We may recall that Egyptian figurines were usually painted with an ochre, more or less dark according to sex, to give a bronze tint to the skin.

The first words of the young man specifically mention the Pharaoh: "To my mare, among Pharaoh's chariots, I would compare you, my love" (1:9). This is a strange comparison which has proved difficult to explain. M. H. Pope has eight pages on this verse.[9] D. Lys[10] thinks that it refers to a luxurious retinue, but he also compares it with texts which mention the horses and chariots from Egypt in the time of Solomon (1 Kgs. 5:6; 10:26,29; 2 Chron. 1:17). In fact this was one of the most conspicuous features of this ostentatious reign; there were 4,000 stalls for horses and chariots and 12,000 horsemen, 2 Chronicles 9:25 states, while 2 Chronicles 1:14 speaks of 1,400 chariots and 12,000 horsemen, making use of the document quoted in 1 Kings 10:26 (the number has been altered in 2 Chronicles 9:25). The Pharaoh Shishak marched on Jerusalem with 1,200 chariots and 60,000 horsemen (2 Chron. 12:2f.). The comparison in Song recalls Isaiah 63:13, repeated in Wisdom 19:9, where the Israelites fleeing Egypt and crossing the Red Sea are compared to horses in the desert. It is well known how much Bedouin poetry likes to compare the loved one to a mare.[11] So there is nothing unusual about Song 1:9; what is more, this text directs our attention right from the beginning toward Egypt.

The same thing is true in regard to the pendants and garlands, the ornaments and necklaces (Song 1:10–11; 4:9). Commentators waver between considering these as descriptions of a horse's harness or of female adornments; Pope does not make up his mind on this. From the el-Amarna period on, paintings and sculptures[12] often depict the heads of people adorned with garlands, braids, wigs, and necklaces, not to mention the breastplates that 4:4 brings to mind: "Your neck is like the tower of David, built in courses; a thousand shields are hung on it, all the bucklers of heroes." We only need think of the bust of Nefertiti! The phrase in 4:3, "Your lips, a scarlet thread," refers to the make-up that Egyptians loved to put on their lips.[13] They also wore perfumed cones on the head, which directs us to 5:13: "His cheeks, beds of spices, clusters delightfully scented." It will be enough to recall some other items common to the Song of Songs and Egyptian love songs: love-sickness, waiting in front of a closed door, snares, pastoral and romantic descriptions with gardens, animals, flowers, fruits, drinks, perfumes, especially myrrh and incense.[14]

The wedding procession described in 3:6–11 would be inspired by a real event. Solomon would have had to go to Gezer for the daughter of Pharaoh to bring her to Jerusalem. It would be normal practice to use a covered palanquin or sedan-chair, frequently pictured in bas-reliefs and paintings in ancient Egypt.[15] G. Gerleman therefore refers to the Opet festival at Luxor when the god Amon came from Karnak to join his consort Mut at Luxor, and to the "Valley Festival" when Amon crossed the Nile to visit the mortuary temples on the west bank of the Nile.[16]

The final words of this section, "on the day of his heart's delight" (3:11) recall the title of the collection of love songs in the Chester Beatty papyrus I which offers so many contacts with the Song: "Beginning of His Heart's Great Joy."[17]

The young girl calls herself the lily of the valleys (2:1), a name immediately repeated by the youth: "Like the lily among the thistles, so is my love among the young women" (2:2). Now the Hebrew word *šwšnh* (lily) is borrowed from the Egyptian *sššn* (old form) or *sšn* which means lotus. It was a woman's name in Egypt, like myrrh, sycamore, flower-bud, lapis lazuli, dove, gazelle.[18] It is not impossible that *šwšnh* was the name of Solomon's wife. In any case, once again we are here directed toward Egypt. The harvesting of lotuses in the Nile marshes depicted in Egyptian paintings[19] illustrates well 6:2: "My beloved has gone down to his garden . . . to gather lilies." It has been noted that going through the marshes to gather papyrus could assume, in the Middle Empire, an erotic feature. In the fragment of "The Story of a Herdsman," a woman, perhaps the goddess Hathor, tries to seduce a shepherd near a papyrus marsh.[20]

In the first praise the youth makes of his beloved, he calls her "his sister" (4:9,10,12; 5:1–2). Such an appellation is common in Egyptian love songs.[21] Just as in the first praise (4:12–5:1), these Egyptian love songs also make great use of the garden theme, mentioning pomegranates, incense trees, aromatic plants; moreover, all these are many times depicted in Egyptian painting. The same thing is true of the love apples or mandrakes (Song 7:14).[22]

The two winds, from the north and from the south (4:16), are the two prevailing winds in the Nile Valley, but not in Palestine. They are met again in Ecclesiastes (1:6): "Southward goes the wind, then turns to the north," and even in Sirach (43:16–17). The sages of Israel are here dependent on the Egyptian world.[23]

According to G. Gerleman, the description of the young man by his loved one (5:10–16) would contain several ideas dependent on Egyptian polychrome statuary.[24] He compares the phrase "his hands, gold sockets" (5:14) to a detail of Egyptian gates: the lower hinge, triangular in shape, supported the weight of the gate, while the upper hinge was cylindrical and resembled a finger.[25] We should note that the Hebrew word *ketem*, "gold" (5:11) is borrowed from Egyptian. "Gold, it is the flesh of the gods," states an Egyptian text.[26] In verse 14 the belly of the youth is said to be a block of ivory; now, in Egypt, blocks of ivory or of metal were often round or oval with a hole in the middle. The word *šeš*, "alabaster" (5:15), which in Hebrew occurs only here, comes from the Egyptian *shš/shšt*.[27] In verse 15, the legs are "columns of alabaster, set on *pedestals* of pure gold." We are therefore in the presence of a veritable statue, according to G. Gerleman. This is an interesting suggestion that once again orients us toward ancient Egypt. It is true that J. B. White[28] thinks that this hypothesis gets us no place, but he still acknowledges the influence of Egyptian love songs on the Song.

We should take note too of a remark of G. Gerleman on 7:3, which he translated "Your navel, a rounded cup." The navel of Egyptian statues is generally made like a bowl turned on its side, a round hole.[29] If this is so, the translation sometimes proposed, namely, "vulva" for the Hebrew *shr(r)*[30] would have no foundation. The same word designates the umbilical cord in Ezekiel 16:4. However, as P. Grelot suggests (*RB* 90, 1983, p. 583), it could be a euphemism for the pubic triangle, always prominently featured on statues and other images of females in the ancient Near East. The allusion is then discreetly modest and could be translated "lap" (*giron*), instead of "navel" (*nombril*). No allusion is made to male genitals in 5:10–16.

It has been suggested that the enigmatic Amminadib of 6:12 be understood as the Palestinian replica of Prince Mehy, a sort of Don Juan of Egyptian love songs: he moved about in a chariot and meddled in the love affairs of others. However, M. Pope is right in thinking that this Prince Mehy is not the *deus ex machina* to make this difficult passage in 6:12 understandable to us.[31] Another solution will be proposed later on in chapter VII.

Ancient Egypt always appreciated the beauty of human beings and nature. The admirable art from Amarna proves the aesthetic sense of these artists in the Nile Valley who had nothing to learn from foreigners. All through Egyptian history artistic masterpieces multiplied. The same love of beauty manifested itself in literature and religion. Egyptian hymns celebrate over and over again the beauty of divine beings, just as love songs celebrate the beauty of human beings. It is not the same in the Old Testament where the beauty of God is rarely brought up (Is. 33:17),[32] and the same is true in regard to the messianic King (Ps. 45:3). As we might expect, it is in the Song of Songs that the root *yfh*, "to be beautiful," is most often used: eleven times, compared to twenty-eight in the rest of the Old Testament. G. Gerleman[33] observes that this root appears again twelve times in narratives attributed to the "J" tradition and those dealing with the reigns of David and Solomon. Thus there is mention of the beauty of Sarah (Gen. 12:11), Rebekah (Gen.

24:16), Rachel (Gen. 29:17), Joseph (Gen. 39:6), David (1 Sam. 16:12; 17:42), Abigail (1 Sam. 25:3), Bathsheba (2 Sam. 11:2), Absalom (2 Sam. 14:25), his sister Tamar (2 Sam. 13:1) and his daughter Tamar (2 Sam. 14:27), and Abishag (1 Kgs. 1:3). Here again we are led to the beginning of the monarchy. It is only in passing that Amos speaks of beautiful young girls (8:13). It will be after the Exile that the sages again develop the theme of feminine beauty (Prov. 5:19; 11:22; 31:30; Job 42:15; Sirach 26:13ff; Esther; Judith; Susanna); however, they also speak of its dangers. As G. von Rad emphasizes, such beauty is especially looked on as something functional, differing in this from the plastic ideal of the Egyptians.[34]

Finally, Egypt is the homeland of allegory, if we accept the opinion of J. G. Griffith, an Egyptologist.[35] He gathers together an impressive collection of fables, riddles, centos in Egyptian tales and novels. This allegorical literature underwent a great development in the Hellenistic period; it exerted a considerable influence on writers and philosophers of Greece and of the ancient world. It is not at all astonishing that such an influence was also felt quite early in neighboring Palestine, especially in literary circles in Jerusalem, quite open to the pagan world in spite of resistance from the religious authorities.

Beginning with the ninth century, perhaps even in the Mosaic period (thirteenth century), scholars, poets and singers from the banks of the Nile must have acquainted the Israelites with the love songs of their country. At the court of Solomon and his Egyptian wife, these poems must have been recited and sung, probably in Hebrew translation. In this way they became little by little an integral part of the literary and musical inheritance of the Hebrew people, as was the case for wisdom writings (Amenophis, etc.). It is in this way that the song of the vineyard (Isaiah 5:1ff.) could begin with an allusion to love. Marriage celebrations were always the occasion for songs, dances and music (Ez. 33:32; Ps. 78:63; 1 Macc. 9:39–41). Jeremiah speaks several times of sounds of joy and happiness, of the voices of bride and bridegroom (7:34; 16:9; 25:10; 33:11; cf Bar. 2:23). These biblical references from before or after the Babylonian Exile allow us to assume the transmission from century to century of love songs, of which several could be inspired by Egyptian models.

Besides references to various oriental customs connected with marriage, there has been no lack of comparisons of the Song with the ancient fertility rites of the sacred marriage, and even with prostitution—not only sacred, but also profane. The Bible occasionally alludes to all these practices.[36] An attempt has therefore been made to locate the prehistory of the Song in this particular ambience, known from the earliest times in the ancient East.[37] But it must be recognized that there is question here of a hypothetical background and in any case one that is completely demythologized by the time of the final composition of the Song, in the Second Temple period.

In fact, in the Persian period an inspired poet selected old love songs of Egyptian origin and incorporated them, along with a lot of other material of varying background, into the original poetical work destined for Jewish believers of the time. Perfectly cognizant of the history and traditions of their people, the faithful of YHWH needed at that time to be stimulated and strengthened in their messianic expectations which were in danger of weakening and collapsing, because of the apparently indefinite delay in the coming of the new Solomon, son of David. It is consequently understandable how certain parts of the Song, which doubtless originally had only an erotic meaning, acquired a new, more usual biblical sense, by reason of their incorporation into a book where they expressed the mutual love of the new Solomon, the expected Messiah, and his promised bride, the daughter of Zion.

*

*   *

---

[1] This marriage would be altogether exceptional, since the Pharaohs did not marry their daughters to foreigners, as Amenophis III wrote to the Babylonian king, Kadash-man-Enlil I, around 1400 BCE (Letter 4 from el-Amarna, lines 6–7). Cf. A. Malamat, "The Kingdom of David and Solomon in its Contact with Egypt and Aram Naharaim," *BA* 21 (1958), p. 98; *ibid.*, 30 (1967), p. 42. In regard to the twenty-first dynasty, see E. F. Wente, "On the Chronology of the Twenty-first Dynasty," *JNES* 22 (1967), pp. 155–76.

[2] This marriage confirmed a treaty with the Pharaoh in which Gezer along with part of the conquered territory of Philistia was handed over to Solomon (cf. A. Malamat, "Aspects of the Foreign Policies of David and Solomon," *JNES* 22 [1963], pp. 8–17). E. W. Heaton could even refer to Solomon as a Pharaoh of Israel (*Solomon's New Men. The Emergence of Ancient Israel as a National State*, London, 1977, pp. 28–30).

[3] From the time of the New Empire, the queen of Egypt had her own palace. It was now the same at Jerusalem. It should be noted that Moses, saved at birth by Pharaoh's daughter (Ex. 2:10), married a Cushite woman (Num. 12:1).

[4] Cf. R. DE VAUX, "Titres et fonctionnaires égyptiens à la cour de David et de Salomon," *RB* 48 (1939), pp. 399–405; T. N. D. METTINGER, *Solomonic State Officials. A Study of the Civil Government Officials of the Israelite Monarchy*, Lund,

1971; A. R. Green, "Israelite Influence at Sheshak's Court," *BASOR* 233 (1979), p. 59.

G. MASPÉRO, "Les chants d'amour du papyrus de Turin et du papyrus Harris n. 500," *JA* 8 (1883), pp. 5–47. He concludes: "It would be profitable then to compare the Song and Egyptian love songs; this would perhaps throw light on certain passages that have been unclear on both sides. However, this is a task that I willingly leave to someone more competent than I; I have done enough for now in providing a part of the material needed by whoever wishes to undertake the task."

[5] In addition to those already listed in Robert-Tournay, pp. 340–52, the following may be consulted: J. B. WHITE, *A Study of the Language of Love in the Song of Songs and Ancient Egyptian Poetry* (SBL DS 38, 1978), Missoula, Montana; see also POPE, *passim*; M. V. FOX, "The Cairo Love Songs," *JAOS* 100 (1980), pp. 101–09; V. L. DAVIS, "Remarks on Michael V. Fox's "The Cairo Love Songs,' " *ibid.*, pp. 111–14; K. PETRÁČEK, "Die Tradition der erotischen Poesie im Nahen Orient und ihre Ausmündung im die romanische Lyrik," *Festschrift Lubor Matouš*, hrsg. B. Hruska–G. Komoróczy, 1979, pp. 201–09.

[7] MIGNE, *Patrologia Graeca*, vol. 66, col. 699–700.

[8] *Op. cit.*, pp. 306–17. Another attempt at an explanation is given by J. CHERYL EXUM, "Asserative *'al* in Canticles 1, 6?" *Bib* 62 (1981), pp. 416–19. In v. 6 the verb *šzf* could be translated by "perceive, discover," as in Job 20:9 and 28:7 (the only other occurrences).

[9] *Op. cit.*, pp. 336–43. O. LORETZ suggests the omission of "to the chariots of Pharaoh" as an addition ("Die Stute im der Kavallerie des Pharao, HL I, 9," *UF* 10 [1978], pp. 440–41).

[10] *Op. cit.*, p. 82.

[11] Cf. G. DALMAN, *Palästinische Diwan*, Leipzig, 1901, pp. 319, 327.

[12] Cf. J. VANDIER, *Manuel d'Archéologie égyptienne*, III, 1958, pp. 491ff; IV, 1964, pp. 30, 172ff.

[13] *ANEP*, 1954, p. 23, fig. 78.

[14] On myrrh, cf. O. LORETZ, *Studien zur althebräischen Poesie, I, Das althebräische Liebeslied* (AOAT 14/1, 1971), p. 10. On perfumes, cf. E. COTHENET, art. "Parfums," *DBSup* 6 (1960), col. 1304–1306. On the "house of wine" ("wine nook") (2:4), cf. M. V. Fox, "Scholia to Canticles," *VT* 33 (1983), pp. 201–02.

[15] Cf. J. VANDIER, *op. cit.*, IV, pp. 328–63.

[16] Cf. POPE, p. 428; G. GERLEMAN, *Ruth. Das Hohelied*, 1965, p. 136.

[17] Cf. P. GILBERT, "Le grand poème d'amour du papyrus Chester Beatty I," *CEg*, 17, n. 34 (1942), pp. 185–98; ROBERT-TOURNAY, pp. 341–43; J. B. WHITE, *op. cit.*, pp. 177–81.

[18] Cf. S. SCHOTT, *Les chants d'amour de l'Égypte ancienne*, Paris, 1956, pp. 116, 178 and note 42; H. RANKE, *Die ägyptische Personennamen*, 1935, pp. 297–98; ROBERT-TOURNAY, p. 436.

[19] Cf. C. VANDIER, *op. cit.*, V (1969), pp. 453–56; also see p. 64.

[20] Cf. J. B. WHITE, *op. cit.*, p. 73; A. HERRMANN, *Altägyptische Liebesdichtung*, Wiesbaden, 1959, pp. 17–19.

[21] Cf. LYS, pp. 181–182; A. BARUCQ and F. DAUMAS, *Hymnes et prières de l'Égypte ancienne* (LAPO 10), Paris, 1980, p. 442, note g.

[22] Cf. S. SCHOTT, *op. cit.*, p. 47, figure 21 (Thebes, tomb 1).

[23] The wind from the south is mentioned again in Ps. 78:26 and Zech. 9:14 (a text that might depend on Hab. 3:3).

[24] *Op. cit.*, pp. 68–72.

[25] *Ibidem*, p. 176.

[26] Quoted by F. DAUMAS, *Les Mammisiss des temples égyptiens. Études d'archéologie et d'histoire religieuse*, Paris, 1958, p. 7; ID., "La valeur de l'or dans la pensée égyptienne," *RHR* 149 (1956), pp. 1–17; A. BARUCQ-F. DAUMAS, *Hymnes et prières* . . . , p. 264.

[27] In Egyptian, alabaster is also called *bj.t*, corresponding to the Hebrew *bht* (Esther 1:6, the only occurrence). A comparison could be made of *nidgālôt* (6:4–10) with the Egyptian word *dgr*, "flag, detachment," from which we get the translation "battalions, armies." S. D. GOITEIN proposes another translation, "splendid like the brilliant stars": " *'ăyummâ kannidgālôt* (Song of Songs VI, 10). 'Splendid like the Brilliant Stars,' " *JSS* 10 (1965), pp. 220–21.

[28] J. B. WHITE, *op. cit.*, p. 197.

[29] Cf. *op. cit.*, p. 197.

[30] As in LYS, p. 258; E.-M. LAPERROUSAZ, *REA* 73 (1971), pp. 372–73 and *REJ* 133 (1974), pp. 2–4; POPE, p. 617.

[31] Cf. *op. cit.*, p. 589; P. S. SMITTER, "Prince Mehy of the Love Songs," *JEA* 34 (1948), p. 116; see *JB*, 2nd. edition, 1985, p. 1039, note h.

[32] Unless *tôb* is translated by "beautiful," as for example in Gen. 6:2 (the daughters of men who were beautiful), or certain words like *n'm* (Pss. 90:17; 135:3) are given this shade of meaning. Such is the case for the name 'Elnā'am (1 Chron. 11:46). In connection with Is. 33:17, H. WILDBERGER (*Jesaja*, X, 16, p. 1315) quotes several Egyptian hymns.

[33] *Op. cit.*, p. 74. He also notes that the root *'hb*, "to love" in the physical, erotic sense is found seven times in Song, eleven times in the narratives of the Yahwist tradition and the traditions in the books of Samuel, out of a total of about thirty occurrences in the Old Testament.

34 This is the way the beauty of Zion, of the people of Israel, etc., is referred to (cf. Pss. 48:3; 50:2; Zech. 9:16; Bar. 5:1; Ez. 16:13–15; etc.). See G. von RAD, *Theology of the Old Testament* I, pp. 362, 365. "Sacral" beauty is the matter being emphasized (cf. c. WESTERMANN, "Das Schöne im A.T.," *Beiträge A.T. Theologie–Festschrift W. Zimmerli, Göttingen*, 1977, pp. 479–97).

35 "Allegory in Greece and Egypt," *JEA* 53 (1967), pp. 78–102; this article is summarized in "The Tradition of Allegory in Egypt," *Religions en Égypte hellénistique et romaine*, Colloque de Strasbourg (1967), Paris, P.U.F., 1969, pp. 45–57.

36 Gen 38:21; Deut. 23:18; 1 Kgs. 14:24; 15:12; 22:47; 2 Kgs 23:7; Hos. 2:4; 4:14; Job 36:14.

37 Cf. O. LORETZ, "Der erste 'Sitz im Leben' des Hohenliedes," *Zur Rettung des Feuers. Solidaritätsschrift für Kuno Füssel* (Christen für den Sozialismus, Gruppe Münster, Hamburger Str. 40), 1981, pp. 32–39; O. KEEL, "Zeichen der Verbundenheit . . . ," *Mélanges D. Barthélemy* (OBO 38, 1981), Freiburg, pp. 197–209. The verb "to come up" (Song 6:10) has the meaning "to look out the window" in Jgs. 5:28 and Prov. 7:6 (an iconographic theme frequently depicted on oriental ivories). In regard to the Sumerian myth of the hierogamy or sacred marriage between Dumuzi and Inanna (Tammuz and Ishtar) and certain parallels with the Song, see ROBERT-TOURNAY, pp. 352–76 and S. N. KRAMER, *The Sacred Marriage. Rite, Aspects of Faith, Myth and Ritual in Ancient Sumer*, Indiana Univ. Press, Bloomington & London, 1969, pp. 85–106 and 352–76.

Chapter Four

"My Beloved Who Sleeps and Whom I Seek"

Abbé Rupert explained in the twelfth century that the Song of Songs owed its name to the presence of the refrain: "I put you under oath, daughters of Jerusalem . . . do not rouse, do not awaken Love before it so desires" (2:7; 3:5; 8:4).[1] The first words of this refrain are repeated in 5:8: "I put you under oath, daughters of Jerusalem . . . "; however, the sequel is about the search for the young man: "If you find my beloved, what must you tell him? That I am sick from love." This last word, "love," is not preceded here by the article as it was in the refrain and as it will be at the end of the poem (8:7); the article is omitted also in the other occurrences of the word "love" (2:4,5; 3:10; 7:7 and 8:6). But grammar alone cannot provide us with a definitive answer on the meaning of the word "love" in the awakening refrain. Many exegetes see here a poetic use of an abstract term (*abstractum pro concreto*) to refer to one of the two lovers. Does it refer to the young man or the young woman? Could it not be a question of the reciprocal love of the two young people?

It was inevitable that the word "love," a feminine word in Hebrew, would be applied to the young woman. Several versions (Peshitto, Vetus Latina, Vulgate) translate the abstract word by a feminine participle, "the well-beloved." This interpretation is accepted by a number of modern authors[2] who depend especially on 7:7 where "love, daughter of delights" evidently refers to the young woman.[3] This is how A. Robert, identifying the husband of the Song with YHWH, saw in the awakening refrain a divine call for the conversion of Israel who was still asleep. He compares it to Isaiah 51:17: "Awake, awake! Up you get, Jerusalem," and also 52:1: "Awake, awake! Clothe yourself in strength, Zion." According to A. Robert, the only person in the Song who is presented to us as asleep is the wife, symbol of the Israelite nation, the daughter of Zion.[4] But it does not seem that this interpretation need be accepted in virtue of the Hebrew text.

In fact, in 5:8, quoted above, it is definitely the young woman who speaks of her beloved to the daughters of Jerusalem. It is she too who is looking for her beloved in 3:1–3 and 5:6–7 and not the other way round. We must not forget either that from the beginning of the Song (1:13) the young woman says that her beloved is a sachet of myrrh who passes the night between her breasts. It is he then, and not she, who sleeps. She is awake through the night (3:1) and according to 5:2 is only half asleep: "I sleep, but my heart is awake." It is he that must not be awakened before he wishes. It is he who is "love." Many modern exegetes understand it this way, going back to the King James version.[5]

This theme of the sleep of the young man and of his eventual awakening, after several "quests," is fundamental for the general interpretation of the Song of Songs. It ensures its profound unity and permits the understanding of certain passages which until now have remained obscure and ambiguous. Such would be the case in 8:3ff. where the young woman, who had previously appealed to her beloved, repeats what she had already said in 2:6: "His left hand is under my head and his right embraces me." She continues, repeating the awakening refrain: "I put you under oath, daughters of Jerusalem, do not rouse, do not awaken Love before it so desires."

A new section begins at 8:5 with the question: "Who is this coming up from the desert, leaning on her beloved?" This question is very much like that in 3:6 which introduced the description of the wedding procession of King Solomon: "What is this which comes up from the desert like a column of smoke?" But, in contrast to 3:7: "It is Solomon's litter . . . ," the continuation of 8:5 does not seem to correspond to the initial question. Nevertheless, it must refer to the young woman, as in 6:10, where queens and concubines extol her while saying in a querying tone: "Who is this who comes up as the dawn . . . ?"

The second part of 8:5 is a tristich that produces a certain overemphasis: " . . . there where your mother conceived you, there where she who bore you conceived you." All the verbs have a masculine suffix of the second person which can only refer back to the young man, as in the following verse: "Put me as a seal on *your* heart (masculine suffix)." It is true that the Peshitta has feminine suffixes here which refer then to the young woman; it is she, and not the young man, that they awaken. A. Robert and other exegetes change the Massoretic text to conform to this, in order to make it fit their fundamental thesis: the awakening of the daughter of Zion, namely, her conversion.[6] But we must above all respect the received text: "Under the apple tree[7] I awaken you, there where your mother conceived you, there where she who bore you conceived you."[8] It is definitely the young woman who here awakens her beloved and it is still she who speaks in the following verse. The whole section forms a coherent discourse as 7:10b to 8:4 did before it. And it is always the young woman who speaks. The big difference is that the time of sleep is over for the young man and the moment of his awakening has at last arrived.

This new situation takes on a very special significance if it is applied to the new Solomon, the Messiah expected by Israel. In fact, the story of Solomon's reign, in 1 Kings 3, places right after the account of the marriage to the daughter of Pharaoh the report of the dream at Gibeon when YHWH appeared *by night* to Solomon. He asked God for wisdom and this was given to him, as well as riches and glory. Then Solomon "awoke (*wyqs*) and it had been a dream."[9] Another text also speaks of Solomon's dream, if we give credence to the title of Psalm 127 (a postexilic psalm), "Of

Solomon," and the allusion in verse 2 to the builder of the temple of YHWH ("If the Lord does not build the house . . . "): "In vain you get up early and put off going to bed, sweating to make a living: he gives as much[10] to his beloved in sleep." Solomon is at the same time Jedidiah, "the beloved of YHWH" (2 Sam. 12:25), and the recipient of the dream at Gibeon. This passage in the Psalm is a good illustration of the tradition that developed in Israel in regard to Solomon. 1 Kgs. 5:12 attributes 1,005 songs to him and Sirach (47:17) says that these songs were the admiration of the world.

It was natural to evoke the delay in the coming of the new Solomon, the Messiah so much awaited, under the poetic image of sleep. All the more so, as this image had become a current anthropomorphism to reproach God for his silence and his apparent lack of activity on behalf of his unfortunate people: "Awake, my God" (Ps. 7:7); "Awake, get up" (Ps. 35:23); "Get up! Why are you asleep, Lord? Wake up. . . . Why do you hide your face?" (Ps. 44:24–25); "Wake up . . . " (Ps. 59:5); "The Lord awakes like a sleeper" (Ps. 78:65). God remains hidden and as if away (Ps. 89:47; Is. 45:15).[11] If it is true that YHWH neither sleeps nor slumbers, the guardian of Israel (Ps. 121:4), the psalmist implores him to come: "When will you come to me?" (Ps. 101:2). Isaiah 63:19 is the same: "Oh, that you would tear the heavens open and come down!"

These repeated agonizing appeals for a divine intervention in favor of Jerusalem and Israel in the Second Temple period witness to the ardent desire for the coming of the King Messiah, the new David, the new Solomon. The prophets Haggai and Zechariah had hailed Zerubbabel as the "Branch" of the Davidic dynasty and the restorer of the ruined Temple. But that hope had been disappointed; Zerubbabel had disappeared without a trace; there was silence on the failure of his mission (see pp. 78).

Not only the theme of sleep was completely appropriate for

bringing to mind the delay in the coming of the Messiah so sorrowfully felt by the Jews, but also the theme of absence and that of seeking could be exploited in the same way. Consequently, the two searches (third and sixth poems) by the young woman for her beloved not only revive a characteristic theme of love songs, but they take on a special significance if one thinks of the new Solomon: "I sought the one whom my soul loves" (3:1); "I will look for the one whom my soul loves. I looked for him but did not find him" (3:2); "I found the one my soul loves" (3:4); "I look for him, but do not find him; I call him, but he does not answer" (5:6). In the second attempt to find her beloved, the young woman is wounded by the city guards who take away her cloak (5:7). Lovesick, she describes her beloved *in his absence*. The daughters of Jerusalem then propose that they go with her to look for him (6:1).

A. Robert has set these texts in the biblical perspective of Covenant language. The theme of seeking-finding is used often to describe the reciprocal relationships of Israel and her God, YHWH.[12] It forms an inclusion in the longest psalm, Psalm 119, in verses 2 and 176. It is found also in the first part of Proverbs (1:28; 7:15; 8:17), edited after the return from Exile. It is especially frequent in the second book of Chronicles, not far removed in time from the Song of Songs; its first nine chapters are devoted to the reign of Solomon. We may cite by way of example the exhortation of the prophet Azariah (2 Chron. 15:2ff.) in which the phrase "seek/find God" appears repeatedly right up to the conclusion: "They earnestly *sought* YHWH. So he allowed himself *to be found* by them and he gave them peace on every side" (15:15). However, A. Robert thought it inconceivable that the Messiah could reveal himself and afterward disappear. But he forgets the case of Zerubbabel, governor of Judah, "a Davidic branch," on whom rested for some time the messianic hopes of Israel, but who prematurely disappeared.[13]

This painful memory could have prompted the description of the two "searches" by the young woman for her beloved. This would indirectly lead their minds toward the anxious expectation, always disappointed and unceasingly renewed, of the King promised to the daughter of Zion (cf. Zech. 9:9). Acceptance of such a *double meaning* makes possible a much better explanation of the fact that the young man speaks so rarely: five verses only (1:9–11,15; 2:2) together with two descriptions of his beloved (4:1–15 and 5:1a–e; 6:4–10 and 7:1c–10a). Otherwise, it is the young woman who speaks, along with the daughters of Jerusalem. And we must await the end of the poem for the young woman finally to "awaken"[14] her beloved from his sleep (8:5c); it is she again who pronounces the epilogue of the whole poem, if, as most exegetes do, we consider that 8:8–14 are additions and therefore really afterthoughts.

In this way the Song of Songs can be interpreted, not only as a real love song between two lovers, but also as a nostalgic song which calls for the coming of the new Solomon, the King who will bring peace and happiness to the daughter of Zion. It is he who will be Peace (Micah 5:4)[15] and also Love (cf. 1 Jn. 4:8,16). As for her, the Shulamite, she will be the one who *found* Peace (8:10), but not without suffering from the "guards" (cf. Is. 52:8; 62:6) posted on the "walls" of the "city" (cf. Neh. 7:3). One cannot refrain from thinking here of Jerusalem with her walls rebuilt by Nehemiah. But we must guard against falling into pure and simple allegory.[16] It is the repetition of the verb "find" as well as of the word "peace" in 8:10 that is enough to suggest that this historicizing reading of the Song was not something foreign to the first readers of the booklet, those who were also its first editors, responsible for the community and the people of Israel—and therefore inspired. We cannot neglect this *first* hermeneutical step in regard to the Song of Songs.

✳

✳   ✳

---

1   See p. 40, note 2.

2   Dom Calmet, Renan, Lys, Robert; also BdJ, TOB, etc.

3   As in Syriac and Aquila, the Massoretic text "in the delights" is divided into two words by reading *bat ta'anûgîm*, "daughter of delights" (there would have been a haplography of *taw*).

4   *Op. cit.*, p. 296. I followed this interpretation in *Le Cantique des Cantiques. Commentaire abrégé* (Lire la Bible 9), Paris, 1967, p. 56.

5   Authorized version, 1611. Cf. Grätz, Harper, Zapletal, Gerleman, etc. The Hebrew verb *taḥpaṣ* is in the feminine because the subject *'aḥăbâ* is feminine. Song 1:13 is cited in the *Gemara* in regard to the two arms of the ark protruding (cf. S. LÉGASSE, "Les voiles du Temple de Jérusalem," *RB* 1980, p. 581, note 107).

6   To avoid changing the Hebrew text as A. Robert did, I had proposed explaining the masculine suffixes by supposing that they were intended to suggest seeing in the spouse the group of repatriated Jews (*op. cit.*, p. 149). I now reject that hypothesis.

7   In 2:3 the young woman compared her beloved to an apple tree: "In his shade which I so desire I sit and his fruit is sweet to my taste." In 7:9 the breath of the young woman is compared to the aroma of apples (Hebrew *tappûaḥ*, "apple" is derived from the verb *nāpaḥ*, "to breathe").

8   The Hebrew text reads: "She bore you." The Septuagint reads it as a participle by vocalizing the verb differently.

Note the emphasis on that phrase, with the repetitions of the adverb "there" (cf. p. 48) and of the verb "conceive."

⁹ This episode has been compared to several Egyptian texts, especially the "Sphinx Stela" of Pharaoh Thut-mose IV. Cf. M. GÖRG, *Gott-König-Reden in Israel und Ägypten* (BWANT 105), Kohlhammer, 1975; *ANET*, 1969, p. 449.

¹⁰ *kēn*, "likewise, as well" (cf. Ez. 40:16, etc.). V. HAMP (*Festschrift Ziegler*, II, 1972, pp. 71–79) translates: "To his beloved he justly gives sleep." The word "sleep" has an Aramaic spelling; some consider it an addition. The versions understood it to mean: "Whereas he will give sleep to his friend." M. DAHOOD compares the Syriac and Ethiopic "prosperity," *Or* 94 (1975), pp. 106–08; *VT* 24 (1974), p. 15. Sometimes the word is changed to *šine'an*, "two-fold," as in the Neo-Vulgate. Cf. LEO PERDUE, *Wisdom and Cult* (Missoula, Montana: Scholars Press, 1977), p. 297.

¹¹ In regard to this "sleep" see G. HAURET, *RSR* 34 (1960), pp. 3–6. The prophets have disappeared (Ps. 74:9; 77:9; 1 Macc. 4:46; 9:27; 14:41).

¹² Hos. 2:9; 3:5; 5:6,15; Am. 5:4–6; Jer. 29:13; Is. 45:19; 51:1; 55:6; 65:1; Zech. 8:21–22; Wis. 1:1–2; 6:12–14; Mt. 7:7–8; Jn 1:38–41; 7:34–36. On the theme of seeking-finding, cf. C. WESTERMANN, "Die Begriffe für Fragen und Suchen im A.T.," *Kerygma und Dogma*, 6, Göttingen, 1960; S. WAGNER, art. *bqšh*, *TDNT*, I, pp. 229–41; *drš*, *ibid.*, II, col. 293–307; see the articles assembled in *Quaerere Deum*, Atti delle XXV Settimana biblica (Paideia ed.), 1980, p. 478. The theme seeking-finding occurs in Egyptian prayers. An example would be the prayer of a blind person to the god Amon: "Amon, great Lord for the one who seeks him, if however (?) one finds

him" (A. BARUCQ and F. DAUMAS, *Hymnes et Prières* . . . , 1980, p. 206, line 25).

[13] A. ROBERT had mentioned this episode in passing; I had suggested a possible allusion in Song 5:6 (ROBERT-TOURNAY, p. 445 in regard to p. 204). Nehemiah (5:15) says that the preceding governors had put a heavy burden on the people; we know from seals the names of three governors after Zerubbabel: *'lntn, yhw'zr, 'hzy* (N. AVIGAD, "Bullae and Seals from Post-exilic Judean Archive,") *Qedem* 4 (1976).

[14] The Hebrew verb is in the perfect as are the following verbs. But the form *qāṭal* can be used of an instantaneous action which happens at the very moment of speaking. Nearly all the examples are in the first person, as is the case here (cf. JOÜON, 112f).

[15] B. RENAUD, chooses the simplest translation: "And that will be peace" (*La formation du livre de Michée*, Paris, 1977, p. 234).

[16] Cyril of Alexandria sees in Song 3:1 an allusion to the women who looked for Jesus on Easter morning (*Patr. Graeca*, 69, col. 1285). A. FEUILLET also compares it to the episode of the disciples of Emmaus ("La recherche du Christ dans la nouvelle Alliance d'après la christophanie de Jo. 20:11–18," *L'homme devant Dieu. Mélanges H. de Lubac. Exégèse et Patristique*, Paris, Aubier, 1964, pp. 93–112). He also compares Rev. 3:20 and Song 5:1–2 and Rev. 12:1ff. and Song 6:10 (*Études d'exégèse et de théologie biblique. Ancien Testament*, Paris, 1975, pp. 333–61, and before that in RSR 49 (1961), pp. 321–53).

Chapter Five

LOVE STRONG AS DEATH

*B*efore we study in detail several difficult passages in the Song of Songs, it would be advisable to direct our attention to the epilogue (8:5–7), as we have done for the prologue (pp. 43ff.). It is not unreasonable to think that, as happened in the case of the prologue, these concluding verses will provide us with some insight on the profound meaning of the Song as a biblical writing, read as such by the community of believing Jews, the "poor of YHWH." We have already seen how the personage of Solomon, so questionable for the narrator of the book of Kings and later on for the sages of Israel (Ecclesiastes 1 and 2; Sirach 51:13f.), not to mention Nehemiah 13:26, happens to be idealized in the Song just as in the book of Chronicles. He has even become the type of the anxiously awaited King-Messiah and embodies in himself the ideal of peace and prosperity promised for centuries to Israel. Consequently, it is in no way surprising that the final part of the Song possesses a completely biblical flavor.

Such is the case in verse 6. Awakened by his loved one, the young man listens to the final request she makes of him: "Put me as a seal on your heart, as a seal on your arm." This text has been compared to a passage in the seventh poem of Cairo ostracon no. 25218: "The young man cries out: 'Oh, that I might be the seal that she wears on her finger!' "[1] The Hebrew word *ḥtm*, "seal" is definitely a borrowing from Egyptian (the word occurs in the Pyramid Texts). Its equivalent *ṭb't* corresponds in turn to the Egyptian *db'.t*. However, the text of Songs also reminds us of several biblical texts in a very remarkable way.

A. Robert had already compared verse 6 to several deuteronomic texts.[2] But he had not noticed the close contact with the last verse of the book of Haggai (2:23): "I will make you, God says to Zerubbabel, like a seal (or: a signet ring). For it is you I have chosen."[3] The same comparison with identical wording is found in the Song. The verb *śym* is followed by the same object and preceded by the same preposition "like." The seal was carried around the neck (Gen. 38:18) or on the right hand (Jer. 22:24); its purpose was to authenticate documents (1 Kgs. 21:8) inasmuch as it was a sign of ownership. Now God had declared expressly in regard to Jehoiachin: "As I live, even if Coniah, son of Jehoiakim, king of Judah, were the signet ring on my right hand, I would still wrench it off " (Jer 22:24). That oracle is henceforth rescinded by the oracle using the same terms and addressed by Haggai (2:23) to Zerubbabel, son of Shealtiel, eldest son of Jehoiachin and descendant of David and of Solomon. In Zechariah 3:8 (cf. 6:12) God calls Zerubbabel "my servant the Branch," a messianic title going back to Jeremiah 23:5 and 33:15 (cf. already Isaiah 11:1–2). Indeed, it is the Davidic Zerubbabel who should rebuild the Temple (Ezra 5:2ff.); wearing the royal insignia, he will sit on his throne and rule (Zech. 6:13). Unfortunately, the prince on whom all the hopes of the returnees rested disappeared in 515 without a whimper, put to death or simply deposed by the Persian authorities. It has already been noted above (p. 72) that the two descriptions of the search for the beloved in the third and sixth poems of the Song could recall this sad event.

H. Cazelles[4] has compared 8:5 with Isaiah 66:7 where the mother, Zion, gives birth to a male child, the new Israel. Other contacts between these two texts should also be pointed out; they are in fact too numerous to be due to chance.

[7]   Before being in labor, she has given birth (*yldh*),
      before the birth pains (*hbl*) came, she has been de-
      livered of a child.

[8]   Who (*my*) ever heard of such a thing? . . . For
      Zion, scarcely in labor, has brought forth (*yldh*)
      her children . . . !

[10] Rejoice with Jerusalem, make merry with her, all
      you who love her (*'hbyh*) . . .

[11] So that you may be suckled (*tynqw*) and satisfied
      from her consoling breast (*mšd*). . . .

[12] . . . Look I am going to have peace (*šlwm;* cf.
      Song 8:10) flow toward her like a river (*knhr*), and
      as a stream overflowing (*šwtf,* "inundating"), the
      glory of the nations. You will be suckled
      (*wynqtm*). . . .

[13] As a man whom his mother (*'mw*) consoles. . . .

[14] At the sight, your heart (*lbkm*) will rejoice . . .

[15] For see how YHWH comes in fire (*b'š*) . . . to sate
      . . . his threat with flaming fire (*blhby-'š*).

We should note in this passage (v. 10) the two words, "re-
joice, make merry" which are also found in the prologue of the
Song (1:4). As for Isaiah 66:6, it begins with *qôl*, "a voice," like
Song 2:8 and 5:2.[5]

A. Robert had pointed out the contacts between Song 8:7
and Isaiah 43:2: "Should you pass through the waters (*mym*), I
shall be with you and the rivers will not engulf you (*yštfwk*);
should you walk through fire (*'š*), you will not suffer, and the
flame (*lhbh*) will not burn you." But the context in each is different. Besides, it is a well-known fact that the third part of Isaiah
(56–66) often repeats phrases from the second part (40–55).[6] All
these passages moreover are from the period after the Babylonian
Exile and shortly before the time of the final composition of the

Song of Songs. The same is true of Proverbs 6:27–28 where love is again compared with fire, as in Sirach 9:8. Proverbs 6:31b, "he will have to hand over all his family resources" corresponds to Song 8:7b, whose didactic tone has many times been emphasized.[7] A. Robert considered it a sapiential addition which could only refer to the love of YHWH for his spouse, the daughter of Zion. He thought in fact that it was the young man who spoke these words.[8] But it is another matter if it is the young woman who speaks here to her beloved, which we consider to be the case. There is nothing preventing this reflection in 8:7b from being the end of her discourse. The final verb "he would be scorned" forms a sort of inclusion with the end of 8:1, "without the people scorning me." It is the young woman who is the speaker throughout.

In Song 8:6, the phrase "flames of Yah" brings to mind lightning, the fire of YHWH (1 Kgs. 18:38; 2 Kgs. 1:12; Job 1:16). Even if the divine name is only considered to have a superlative use (cf. Jer. 2:31) and is translated "a divine flash of lightning," as in the translation of D. Lys,[9] the parallelism between "love" and "jealousy" directs us to the group of texts which speak of a "jealous" God in the terminology of Covenant.[10] YHWH loves Israel as a spouse, with an eternal love (Jer. 31:3). The conclusion of the Song directs us then toward the traditional biblical theme of the marriage allegory, so frequently developed by the prophets, from Hosea to Ezekiel, as well as by the final part of the book of Isaiah. Already, the repetition of the adverbs, *šām, šammāh*, "there," in 7:13 and 8:5 could call to mind the name of Jerusalem (p. 48); then there is Ezekiel 23:3 where the same repetition appears at the beginning of the symbolic history of Jerusalem and Samaria.[11]

In regard to the "mighty waters," Sheol, and lightning, some are content to refer to certain Canaanite, Mesopotamian and Egyptian texts on mythical chaos, underworld deities, the great god of thunder, the combat of Mot and Ba'al at Ugarit (Ras Shamra), etc. But it must be conceded that all this is "demythologized" in the Song.[12] The expression "mighty waters" is frequently used in the Bible, especially in the postexilic writings; it can refer symbolically to an enemy invasion or to deadly threats. In Song 8:7 it is a question apparently of all the ordeals and attacks imaginable which could come along to overwhelm two people who love each other with a love that is loyal and seeking to be eternal and life-giving.

In Egyptian love songs, the two lovers are called brother and sister. In the Song, the young woman avoids referring to her beloved as "brother"; but she still wishes to be in a position to say to him: "Oh that you were my brother!" (8:1). On the other hand, the young man never fails to speak of his "sister," as we have seen already (p. 58f). This anomaly is easily understandable if the poet is thinking here of a transcendent personage, as the new Solomon will be. It can also be noted that the young woman speaks insistently of the mother of her beloved (8:5), just after having spoken of her own mother (8:1–2). As the mention of Solomon's mother in 3:11 already inclines us to do, it is not out of line to let our thoughts be directed once again here toward the mother of Solomon, Bathsheba (2 Sam. 12:24–25) who successfully contributed to her son Solomon's accession to the throne (1 Kgs. 1:11–21).

To sum up, the epilogue of the Song associates with the lyrics of love didactic speech and certain themes from the prophetic writings. The whole of 8:1–7 appears to be a literary unit separated into two parts by the refrain and spoken entirely by the young woman. In addition to the verbal similarity of the two sections pointed out already, it is appropriate to emphasize the repetition of the key word "love," found already in the refrain of verse 4 and afterward repeated three times in verses 6–7. This is in fact the central theme of the Song. *The epilogue then links up with the prologue* in which the two initial strophes (1:2–3 and 4) each end with the same verb "love."

For anyone concerned about abstract logic, such procedures are disconcerting. Images and symbols follow one another and intermingle as poetical inspiration impells; but the literary treasure of the Israelite sages and prophets is there in the background too. This permits the modern reader to interpret these verses in a polyvalent way, according to a *double entendre*,[13] in the light of other biblical books, and among these books the Song occupies an irreplaceable position.

✳

✳   ✳

[1]   Cf. ROBERT-TOURNAY, p. 349. J. B. WHITE, *op. cit.*, pp. 147–48 (note 48). Analogous desires are found in the Chester Beatty Papyrus (cf. J. B. WHITE, *op. cit.*, pp. 181–82). See also S. SCHOTT, "Wörter für Rollsiegel und Ring," *WZKM* 54 (1957), pp. 117–85. Possibly there is a play on words between *ḥtm*, "seal" and *ḥtn*, "fiancé." In regard to this Chapter V, see R. J. TOURNAY, "The Song of Songs and its Concluding Section," *Immanuel* 10 (1980), Jerusalem, pp. 5–13.

[2]   He refers to Deut. 6:6–8; 11:18; Ex. 13:9; Jer. 31:33; Prov. 3:3 (*op. cit.*, pp. 299–300).

[3]   The same verb "to choose" is applied to Solomon by the Chronicler (1 Chron. 28:5,10; 29:1).

[4]   In the review of ROBERT-TOURNAY, *Le Cantique des Cantiques*, published in *Bulletin du Comité des Études de la Compagnie de Saint-Sulpice*, nn. 42–43, April–Sept. 1963, p. 214.

5   Note the verb *'ng* in v. 11 of Isaiah 66 and the derivative *t'ngym*
    in Song 7:7.

6   Cf. J. VERMEYLEN, *Du prophète Isaïe a l'apocalyptique*, II, 1978,
    p. 495.

7   A.-M. DUBARLE has already drawn attention to these literary
    and thematic contacts in his article, "L'amour humain
    dans le Cantique des Cantiques," *RB* 61 (1954), p. 80; *ID.*,
    "Le Cantique des Cantiques dans l'exégèse recente," *Aux
    grands carrefours de la révélation et de l'exégèse de l'A.T.* (Re-
    cherches Bibliques VIII, 1966), Desclée de Brouwer, pp.
    147–48. On verse 7, cf. N. J. TROMP, "Wisdom and the
    Canticle, Ct. 8:6c–7b. Text, Character, Message and Im-
    pact," *La Sagesse de l'Ancien Testament*, ed. M. Gilbert
    (BETL 51, 1979), pp. 88–95. See earlier, A. R. JOHNSON,
    "Mashal," *Wisdom in Israel and the Ancient Near East*,
    Festschrift H. H. Rowley (VTSup 3, 1955), pp. 162–69. See
    also M. SADGROVE, "The Song of Songs as Wisdom Lit-
    erature," *Studia Biblica* I (6th Internat. Congress of Bib-
    lical Studies, Oxford, 3–7 April, 1978), Sheffield, 1979,
    pp. 245–48.

8   *Op. cit.*, p. 304.

9   LYS, pp. 289, 292.

10 Cf. B. RENAUD, *Je suis un Dieu Jaloux* (Lectio Divina 36), Paris,
    1963; cf. *RB* 71 (1964), pp. 119–20. We may refer by way
    of example to Zech. 1:14; 8:2; Joel 2:18.

11 The author of Song 6:4 avoids mentioning Samaria and re-
    places it by Tirzah (1 Kgs. 15:21ff.) due to the meaning
    of this name, "Pleasure" (LXX *eudokia*). Cf. Is. 62:4,12;
    Num. 26:33.

[12] Cf. H.-P. MÜLLER, "Die lyrische Reproduktion des Mythischen im Hohenlied," *ZTK* 73 (1976), pp. 23–41.

[13] In his review of POPE's commentary, J. M. SASSON ("On M. H. Pope's Song of Songs," *Maarav* 1/2. 1978–79, pp. 177–96) accepts the *double-entendres* (p. 182) and refers (p. 185) to the exegesis of Ibn Ezra (quoted by POPE, p. 103).

Chapter Six

THE MOUNTAINS OF BETER AND MOUNT MORIAH

*T*he second poem of the Song of Songs (2:8–17) is presented, as is the third (3:1–5), in the form of a discourse by the young woman. However in verses 10–14 she is quoting the words of the beloved. All the commentators have had to face up to the difficulties in trying to give a coherent interpretation of verses 15 and 17. The final word *beter* presents the main difficulty. Let us endeavor to understand it.[1]

Those who see here merely a simple love song propose a symbolic explanation. The "mountains of Beter" are the two breasts of the young woman. The last verse of the Song is used as a comparison: "Flee, my beloved, and be like the gazelle or the young fawn on *the mountains of spices*" (8:14). This verse repeats 2:17, but with some variations; *beter* would have as its equivalent in 8:14 *bōśem*, "spice," a term frequently occurring in the Song.[2] But why would such an obscure term be used in the first passage? St. Jerome considered it a geographical name and transcribed *montes Bether;* several exegetes, such as F.-M. Abel, turn it into a place name, perhaps Bettir, eleven kilometers west of Jerusalem;[3] other localizations have also been proposed. But the Song contains several well-known geographical names. Why would mountains that cannot be identified be mentioned here? Malabathron or betel, a sort of Indian pepper-plant (*pilpēl hôdû* in modern Hebrew), has even been considered.

The best explanation is found in rabbinical writings. They compare Song 2:17 to the narrative in Genesis (15:10ff.) which describes YHWH and Abraham concluding the "covenant between the pieces." This special covenant ritual is mentioned again in the Hebrew text of Jeremiah 34:18: "I am delivering the people who failed to keep the promises that I had them make, who have not honored the terms of the promise that they decided to accept before me, by cutting in two a bull-calf and passing *between the pieces*" (the Septuagint does not have this text!). Those making the agreement in this way called down on themselves the same fate the victim suffered, in case they broke their promises.[4] The Hebrew word *beter*, "a piece cut off," is derived from the verb *btr*, "to share"; this noun in Genesis 15:10 forms a play on words with *bĕrît*, "covenant," inasmuch as these two words are used in the same passage, a few verses apart: "That day YHWH made a covenant with Abram" (Gen. 15:18). Is not every covenant, moreover, a sharing of love or friendship? Following Proverbs 2:17, Malachi 2:14 uses the word *bĕrît* in speaking of marriage.

The classical formula for covenant, "You will be my people and I shall be your God"[5] has been compared to the "belonging" formula of the Song: "My beloved is mine and I am his" (2:16; 6:3 in reverse order; 7:11 partially). In Deuteronomy 26:17–18; Hosea 2:25; Jeremiah 7:23 and 31:33, it is God who is named first; elsewhere, it is the people of Israel. It is possible that the order chosen suggests who took the initiative in the agreement. In Deuteronomy 26:17–18, God goes ahead to conclude the covenant agreement; in Hosea 2:25, out of mercy he reestablishes relations after the wife repents; Jeremiah 31:33 shows God creating a new covenant. In the Song, 6:3 and 7:1 name the young woman first; but in the first occurrence, in 2:16, because the "beloved" has just completed his exhortation, he is placed first; he took the initiative, as God did with respect to Abraham at the time of the covenant between the pieces. Jewish tradition invites us to deepen these contacts between the Song and the narrative of the covenant between God and Abraham.

We may mention some excerpts from the Targums. The

Targum on Song 2:11–12 and 17 makes the comparison with Genesis 15 and adds to it Genesis 22, the narrative of the sacrifice of Isaac, the Akedah: "The years predicted to Abraham *between the pieces* have expired; the time of redemption promised to Abraham our father (has arrived). . . . " "He remembers the covenant that he had sworn with Abraham, Isaac and Jacob . . . and the offering that Abraham had made of Isaac his son on Mount Moriah; but before that, he had made his offerings there, after having them *divided into parts* that were equal."[6] The mountains of *beter* are here identified with Mount Moriah; according to 2 Chronicles 3:1, this mountain is none other than the hill on which the Temple of Jerusalem was built. It is there that rabbinical tradition and, after it, the Muslim tradition situate the sacrifice of Isaac. The Targum also identifies with Moriah the mountain of myrrh and the hill of incense, mentioned in 4:6 (cf. already 3:6): "(Israel crosses the Jordan thanks) to the merit of Abraham who prayed and worshiped before YHWH on Mount Moriah . . . and to the justice of Isaac who was bound on the site of the Temple, called the mountain of incense."[7] In addition to the play on words already mentioned between *beter* and *bĕrît*, there is here a new play on words between *môr*, myrrh and the proper name Moriah.[8] Such methods are customary in the midrashic and haggadic literature; it is not a case here of simple intellectual gymnastics, but a traditional hermeneutical method, especially with regard to the etymology of proper names.

The Targums associate the sacrifice of Isaac, or the Akedah, with the Passover and the covenant between the pieces. This could explain why the Song scroll was at an early date recited by the Jews at the time of the Paschal *seder*, not to mention other reasons for this, such as the allusion that was thought to be seen to the Exodus from Egypt in 1:9, or to the description of springtime in 2:11ff.

Let us quote still more texts taken from various Targums:

The Targum on Exodus 12:42, a passage to which R. Le Déaut gives the title "The Poem of Four Nights": "The second night took place when the Memra (the Word) of the Lord showed itself to Abraham between the pieces."[9]

The Palestinian Targum: "I remember the covenant that I made with Isaac on Mount Moriah and the covenant with Abraham between the pieces."[10]

Targum of Micah 7:20: "You will show mercy to Abraham and to his descendants after him as you swore between the pieces; you will remember on our behalf the Akedah of Isaac who was bound on the altar before you."[11]

Targum of Ezekiel 16:3: "There (in the land of Canaan) I revealed myself to Abraham your father between the pieces and I made known to him that you would go down to Egypt. . . . In the blood of circumcision I will have mercy on you; in the blood of the Passover I will redeem you."[12]

The tradition reflected in all these texts may go far back. We may ask whether it is not possible to find a first echo, at least an indirect one, of this in Song 2:17 and 4:6: "Before the day dawns and the shadows flee. . . . " The mountains of "sharing" (*beter*) correspond then to the mountain of myrrh and the hill of incense (or of frankincense). It is night when the sun has set and in the darkness a smoking firepot and a flaming torch passed *between the pieces* (Genesis 15:17). In precisely the same way, Song 2:17 speaks of shadows and night. It is true that the flight of shadows has been interpreted as if it were dusk when the shadows grow longer on the ground and the wind becomes stronger. But we may also think of early morning and the morning breeze. It is immediately after (3:1) that we find, still during the night, the search for the young man. Certainly, the whole passage could bring to mind the night of Passover, for the offering of the lamb must take place between the two evenings.[13]

The second poem of the Song may also allude to other in-

cidents in the story of Abraham. We may refer first to the phrase
lekî-lāk (2:10–13) which is usually translated "come," like *lĕkâ* in
7:12, because of the context. However, the construction is different. In the following verse (v. 11) we find the same construction as in 2:10 and 13: the same verb *hlk*, with the preposition
lamed and the suffix; there is no problem in translating: "The rain
has gone away." So *lekî-lāk* should mean instead "go away from
there to come toward me, set off to meet me." The same expression in these two verses should be understood in the same way.
There are other verbs for "come" (*bô*; or *'th* as in 4:8). For want
of something better, *lekî-lāk* is here translated as "come away."

Now, the imperative singular of the verb *hlk*, "to go,"[14] followed by *lamed* and a pronominal suffix is met elsewhere only in
two texts, in the story of the patriarch Abraham: (1) Genesis 12:1:
"*Go away* from your country, your family and your father's house
toward the country that I will show you." Here are the first
words that God addresses to the Father of believers, at the dawn
of salvation history. (2) Genesis 22:2: "Take your son, your only
son, Isaac, whom you love; *go away* toward the land of Moriah. . . . " It is the beginning of the story of the sacrifice of Isaac,
called in the rabbinical writings the *Akedah* (a word derived from
the verb *'qd*, "to bind").

The first call to depart is the very first meeting between God
and Abraham; it will be concluded by a covenant. At the time of
the second call to depart, God asks of Abraham that which was
most dear to him in order to realize the mysterious plan of his
Love. And we have there the two parallels to Song 2:10 and 13
where we find once again the allusion to Mount Moriah. We may
also note the repetition of "your country," "the country" in Genesis 12:1, and "in the country," "in our country" in Song 2:12.
There is also the same use of the two verbs "get up" and "go
away" (or "come away") in Genesis 22:3 and Song 2:10 and 13.

Besides, we may wonder whether Song 2:10 and 2:13–14 do

not make a discreet allusion to the beautiful Sarah, the wife of Abraham. Abraham says to Sarah that she is beautiful to look at (*yefat mar'eh*, Genesis 12:11); the Egyptians recognize that she is very beautiful (*yāfâ me'ōd*, Genesis 12:14). Now these words are used by the young man of his well-beloved in Song 2:10 and 13. In verse 14 he adds: "Your face is charming" (*mar'eh*). The beauty of Sarah had become proverbial; the rabbinical writings, the Talmud and the Midrashes all refer to it. The wife of Tobit, Sarah, is also described as a thoughtful, courageous young woman and very charming as well (Tobit 6:12). It is especially in the Aramaic Genesis Apocryphon discovered at Qumran that the beauty of Sarah gives rise to a long description where they find it enough to go over the parts of the body moving from above to below, as in Song 4:1ff.:[15]

[2] (. . .) how splendid and beautiful is the form of her face, and how [3] (. . .) and how soft the hair of her head; how lovely are her eyes and how pleasant is her nose, and all the radiance [4] of her face (. . .)! How lovely is her breast and how beautiful her complexion! Her arms, how beautiful, and her hands, how [5] perfect! And how lovely are her palms, and how long and dainty all the fingers of her hands! Her feet [6], how beautiful! How perfect are her legs.

There are no virgins or brides who enter a bridal chamber more beautiful than she. Indeed, her beauty [7] surpasses that of all women; her beauty is high above all of them. Yet with all this beauty there is much wisdom in her; and all the work of her hands [8] is marvelous.

Let us return to chapter 15 of Genesis. At the end of the chapter there is a list of the inhabitants of Canaan who will be dispossessed by the descendants of Abraham: ten pre-Israelite peoples are named and the list is met again in many texts,[16] but with variations. P. Joüon and G. Ricciotti had already proposed identifying the "little foxes" of Song 2:15 who destroy the vineyards with the Canaanite peoples and neighbors of Israel, the Vineyard of YHWH.[17] A. Robert[18] revived this interpretation which had been mistakenly rejected without sufficient consideration. Profiting from the fall of Jerusalem in 587 and the weakness of the people of Judah, the wicked neighbors of Israel came to pillage and plunder the country. As the book of Lamentations 5:18 says: "The mountain of Zion is desolate: jackals prowl there." We may add Nehemiah 3:35 which quotes a scornful remark of Tobiah of Ammon after the speech of Sanballat, at the time of the reconstruction of the walls of Jerusalem: "If a jackal were to jump on what they are building, it would knock their stone wall down!"

In Song 2:15, the plural in the Received Text, "our vineyards" could be a harmonization with the plural "the vineyards" which precedes it. In fact, many of the manuscripts of the Massoretic text as well as the Vulgate have the singular "our vineyard" here; this agrees with "my own vineyard" in 1:6 or "our land" in 2:12, or again "a vineyard, my vineyard" in 8:11–12. Comparison is called for then with Psalm 80:14 where the psalmist describes how the wild boars of the forests and the beasts of the fields devour the Vineyard Israel. The theme of the flock of Israel devoured by the wild beasts, the Assyrians, the Babylonians and the Egyptians, is found as late as 1 Enoch (89:54ff.). These allegorical developments are therefore traditional.[19]

Of course, the theme of foxes as ravagers of vineyards belongs to world literature. La Fontaine's fable, *The Fox and the Grapes* is well known. On a mosaic at Khirbet el-Mekhayyat,[20] near Mount Nebo, the third row of figures depicts an elderly man in a short sleeveless tunic, tightened at the waist by a cord, wearing thonged sandals, a basket filled with grapes held on his back by a strap which he holds with both hands; he is hurrying while a fox scampers along ahead of him.

However, every Jewish reader of the Song of Songs must have made this comparison, since so many texts call to mind the vineyard of Israel and the destructions it underwent in the course of its history.

Like that of the vineyard, the image of the dove is often a symbolic designation for Israel. Song 2:14 and other references to the dove to allude to the young woman (1:15; 4:1; 5:2,12; 6:9) should bring to mind other biblical texts where the same symbol is found. Hosea 7:11 compares Israel to a silly dove. The psalmists (Pss. 68:14; 74:19) also make use of this comparison; it is the same in a postexilic passage, Hosea 11:11, in regard to the return from Exile: "From the land of Assyria they will come running like doves." This text should be compared to Isaiah 60:8: "They fly like doves to their nests." This image of the dove recurs in 2 Esdras 5:26 and is not unusual in the rabbinical writings.[21] Incidentally, the comparison with a bird is used in Jeremiah 12:9 to recall the raids of the Moabites, Ammonites, and Edomites into Palestine after 587; verse 10 continues: "Many shepherds have laid my vineyard waste, have trampled over my plot of land, reducing the plot of land which was my joy to a deserted wilderness." This is the imagery already mentioned.

It is therefore permitted to go beyond the obvious meaning of the words in this second poem and interpret them in the light of other texts about the story of Abraham or the catastrophe of 587. However, there are certain details that are somewhat ambiguous. Thus the word *zāmîr* (2:12) can have more than one meaning: the pruning of the vineyard (cf. Isaiah 5:6; Leviticus 25:3) or the singing of the turtledove. Despite scholarly studies, it is hard to choose between the two meanings, for they both fit the context.[22] The description relates in fact to springtime in Palestine and not to the autumn. The rains usually end toward the month of April in this country, and that is the time of blossoming[23] for the vineyards.

The expression "he who feeds among the lilies" (2:16 and also 6:3) is also ambiguous. The Septuagint translated: "He made the flock graze" (cf. 1:7). But the Vulgate understood: "He fed among the lilies" (cf. 4:5). This second meaning could have erotic implications; the young man would enjoy the charms of his loved one, compared elsewhere to a lily (2:2) and to an enclosed and fragrant garden (4:14; 5:1; cf. 6:2). M. H. Pope acknowledges such ambiguity.[24] But the phrase "to feed among the lilies" may simply refer to the picking of the lotuses, mentioned in 6:2 and sometimes portrayed on bas-reliefs of ancient Egypt. At Deir el-Gebrawi, men wade in deep water and pull up magnificent lotus stalks, using just one hand. One person is offering the barge captain a superb lotus flower.[25] We will see later (p. 117) that the phrase discussed here can be an allusion to the person of David, the shepherd, ancestor of the Messiah.

A striking example of the application to the Patriarchs of a passage from the Song, around the beginning of the Common Era, is the citation of Song 4:14 in the *Life of Adam and Eve* 43:3,[26] using the same order of the perfumes: nard, saffron, calamus and cinnamon, in regard to Eve and her son Seth. This Hebrew apocryphal work, come down to us in translations, is usually dated between 20 and 70 C.E., since it seems to make an allusion to the construction of the Temple by Herod the Great.[27] We would have here then the oldest witness to the use of the Song by the Jewish people to illustrate the lives of the ancestors of Israel.

We may add that the passage from 2 Esdras, referred to above, has also been compared to the Song of Songs. Before the image of the dove, it also has the images of the vineyard and the lily. A. Feuillet, following R. H. Charles, thinks that the text clearly takes its inspiration from the Song; this would be a valuable testimonial to the allegorical interpretation of the Song, from the end of the first century, almost contemporaneous with the New Testament.[28]

✳

✳   ✳

---

[1]   See already R. TOURNAY, "Abraham et le Cantique des Cantiques," *VT* 25 (1975), pp. 544–52.

[2]   Cf. 4:10,14,16; 5:1,13; 6:2.

[3]   F.-M. ABEL, *Géographie de la Palestine II*, p. 271; POPE, p. 410. Cf. Jos. 15:59 and 1 Chron. 6:44 in LXX, ms. A.

[4]   For details of this ritual, cf. A. de PURY, *Promesse divine et légende cultuelle dans le cycle de Jacob* (Études Bibliques), I, 1975, pp. 313ff. According to E. J. BICKERMANN, the vital breath of the victims would be communicated to the one who passes between them, in this way making his promise stronger and more binding ("Couper une alliance," *Studies in Jewish and Christian History*, Arbeiten zur Geschichte des antiken Judentums und des Christentums, Band 9, Leiden, Brill, 1976, pp. 1–32). P. Amiet compares with this ritual a scene engraved by an Elamite artist: "Two serpents frame a sort of portable dwelling which a woman protects and all this is set between the two halves of a bull cut in two" ("Rois et dieux d'Elam d'après les cachets et les sceaux-cylindres de Suse," *Archéologia* 36 [Sept.–Oct. 1970], p. 24 and fig. 5).

[5]   Cf. A. FEUILLET, "La formule d'appartenance mutuelle (Cant. II, 16)," *RB* 68 (1961), pp. 5–38. See N. LOHFINK, "Deut. 26:17–19 und die Bundesformel," *ZKTh* 91 (1959), pp.

517–53 (cf. Ex. 6:7; Lev. 26:12; etc.). Compare 2 Chron. 15:2: "YHWH is with you when you are with him."

6   Cf. R. LE DÉAUT, *La nuit pascale* (AnBib 22, 1963), Rome, pp. 144 and 175. He mentions this comparison with Song 2:17 on pages 107 and 136 and quotes A. FEUILLET, *RB* 68 (1961), pp. 30–31; see ROBERT-TOURNAY, p. 128. SH. YEIVIN has proposed a Hurrian etymology for the word Moriah in *Tarbiz* 40 (1970), p. 1 (summary in English).

7   Cf. R. LE DÉAUT, *op. cit.*, pp. 175–76; see also pp. 110–11, 161 and 186.

8   Cf. ROLF PETER SCHMITZ, "Aqedot Jishaq. Die Mittelalterliche Jüdische Auslegungen von Genesis 22 im ihren Hauptlinien," *Judaistiche Texte und Studien*, B. 4, 1979, Hildesheim-New York, pp. 43–44. Nachmanides mentions 4:6 in regard to Moriah. See ROBERT-TOURNAY, p. 168. In Zeph. 3:1 there would be an analogous play on words on Jerusalem the rebel, *moreah* (cf. L. SABOTKA, *Zephania*, Rome, 1972, p. 103).

9   Cf. R. LE DÉAUT, *op. cit.*, p. 135.

10 *Ibid.*, p. 174.

11 *Ibid.*, p. 176, note 116.

12 *Ibid.*, p. 144.

13 *Ibid.*, p. 143 and note 24. J. SMIT SIBINGA compared 2 Peter 1:19 with Song 2:17 ("Une citation du Cantique dans la Secunda Petri," *RB* 73 [1966], pp. 107–19).

14 There is a plural in Jos. 22:4: "Go back" (the Transjordanian tribes are being addressed). The use of the *lamed* after a verb is debated; cf. T. MURAOKA, "On the so-called Dativus Ethicus in Hebrew," *JTS NS* 29 (1978), pp. 495–98. It is a question of a reflexive or centripetal dative. JOÜON, n. 133d, speaks of a *dativus commodi* (cf. Song 2:10,17). The verb *hlk* means "to go" in Song 4:6; 6:1; 7:10,12; 1 Kgs. 1:13; Gen. 22:5; etc.

15 ROBERT-TOURNAY, p. 388; J. A. FITZMYER, *The Genesis Apocryphon of Qumran Cave 1* (Biblica et Orientalia 18, 1966), Rome, pp. 54–55, 106–11; J. C. VANDERKAM considers it a poem in nine stanzas ("The Poetry of lQApGen, XX, 2–8a, *RevQ* 37 (1979), pp. 57–66).

16 Ex. 3:8,17; 13:5; 23:33; 33:2; Deut. 7:1; 20:17; Jos. 3:10; 9:1; 11:3; 12:8; 24:11; Jgs. 3:5; 1 Kgs. 9:20; Ezra 9:1; Neh. 9:8; 2 Chron. 8:7.

17 Hos. 10:1; Is. 5:1ff; Jer. 2:21; 5:10; 6:9; 12:10; Ez. 15:1ff; 17:6ff; 19:10ff; Ps. 80:9ff; Is. 27:2ff; Deut. 32:32; Sirach 24:17; etc. The theme is taken up again in the New Testament: Mt. 21:33ff; Jn. 15:1ff.

18 *Op. cit.*, p. 124. Other symbolic uses: Ez. 13:4 (the prophets); Lk. 13:32 (Herod).

19 Cf. Hos. 2:14; Jer. 5:17; 8:13; 12:9; Ez. 24:8,25; etc. See A. FEUILLET, *RB* 68 (1961), pp. 27–28.

20 P. LEMAIRE, "Mosaïques et inscriptions d'el-Meḥayet," *RB* 43 (1934), p. 390 and plate XXIV, 2.

21 STRACK-BILLERBECK, *Kommentar zum Neuen Testament aus Talmud und Midrash*, I, Munich, 1922, pp. 123–24. Cf. R. TOURNAY, "Le psaume LXVIII et le livre des Juges," *RB* 66 (1959), p. 383; *Les Psaumes (BdJ)*, 3rd ed., 1964, p. 291, note f. It is possible that this image of the dove demythologizes that of the dove of the goddess Anat. E. LIPÍNSKI ("La colombe du Ps. LXVIII 14," *VT* 23 (1973), pp. 365–68) proposes a new interpretation, reading *ml'kym*, "the messengers"; but it is not necessary to correct the received text. A. FEUILLET sees in the dove at the baptism of Jesus some kind of reference to the new Israel ("Le Symbolisme de la colombe dans les récits évangeliques du Baptême," *RSR* 46 (1958), pp. 524–44.).

22 Cf. POPE, p. 396; C. GORDON, "New Directions," *Naphtali Lewis Festschrift*, *BASP* 15 (1978), p. 59; A. LEMAIRE, "Za-

mir dans la tablette de Gézer et le Cantique des Cantiques," *VT* 25 (1975), pp. 15–26; he proposes translating
zāmîr by "vintage."

[23] The Hebrew *sĕmādar* (Song 2:13,15; 7:13) corresponds to Aramaic *sĕmādrā*; it refers to the bud of a flower which
opens, according to 7:13; Cf. SH. AHITUV, "The Meaning
of Semadar," *Leshonenu* 39 (1974–75), pp. 37–40; N. von
SODEN, *Akkadisches Handwörterbuch*, 1016 b.

[24] *Op. cit.,* pp. 405–06. In regard to this refrain, cf. A. FEUILLET,
RB 68 (1961), pp. 7–9; J. ANGÉNIEUX, "Structure du Cantique des Cantiques," *ETL* 52 (1965), p. 116.

[25] See pp. 58 and 117; J. VANDIER, *Manuel . . .* , V, 1969, pp.
453ff.

[26] Cf. ELIO PIATELLI, "Vita Adae et Evae," *Annuario di Studi
Ebraici*, 1968–69, pp. 9–23; UGO BIANCHI, "La rédemp-
tion dans les livres d'Adam," *Numen* 18 (1971), pp. 1–8;
LYS, p. 194.

[27] "The new construction of the house of God, which will be
more exalted than in the past" (29:6). It is true that it
could merely be question here of messianic times.

[28] A. FEUILLET, "Le symbolisme de la colombe . . . ," *RSR* 46
(1968), pp. 535–36; L. GRY, *Les dires prophétiques d'Esdras*,
Paris, 1938, I, pp. 63–67.

Chapter Seven

THE CHARIOTS OF AMINADAB

Verse 12 of chapter 6 of the Song of Songs is generally considered the most difficult to understand of the whole booklet. There are even those who want to omit it as a gloss[1] or who consider it as corrupted beyond recovery. Such solutions are too much the easy way out. It has also been imagined that a scribe would have admitted to himself his embarrassment, by writing at the beginning: "I do not know," in other words, "I don't understand."[2] It would be tedious to recall here all the textual emendations that have been proposed, for none of them is convincing. Following Grätz, Zapletal and Galling, D. Lys thinks up the root *rkk* and reads *morek bat nadib*. He therefore translates: "I do not know my own self: it makes me timid, a daughter of noble people."[3] The root *brk* has also been considered; J. B. White proposes *mĕbōreket*, "the blessed."[4] M. Bogaert reads *śamtanî* and *'immî;* he translates: "I do not know, my soul, you have paid me the honor of (your) palanquins."[5] For other exegetes, the word *nādîb*, "prince," would allude to Prince Mehy, a sort of Don Juan of Egyptian love songs, especially in Harris papyrus 500. We have referred to this above (pp. 60; 64, n. 5); G. Gerleman thinks it is a literary caricature (a hypothesis frequently proposed) and an imitation of the theme of Prince Mehy who rode around in a chariot.[6] In any case there is recourse to a paraphrase. Hence M. H. Pope: "Unaware I was set in the chariot with the prince."[7] Or again G. R. Driver: "She made me feel more than a prince reigning over the myriads of his people."[8]

The Greek version, the Septuagint, translates: "My soul did

not know; it made of me the chariots of Aminadab." Rashi follows
the Massoretic punctuation which also divides after "I did not
know"; he then paraphrases: "My soul made me be chariots for
the princes of the rest of the nations to ride upon." It would involve then the subjection of Israel to foreigners.

It is a good idea to analyze in detail the whole verse. The
word *nefeš* should have the same meaning here as in 1:7 and 3:1–
4 where *nafšî* means "my desire," "my heart." The verb *śym* is
constructed with a double accusative, which frequently is the
case elsewhere, especially in the Psalms.[9] But what is meant by
the compound word, *'ammî-nādîb*, at the end of the sentence? Literally it means "my noble people," or "my generous people." The
term *nādîb* is used a little later (7:2) to describe the young woman:
bat-nādîb, called also *šûlammît* in 7:1 (twice), where the verb "come
back" is repeated four times. These repetitions are not a matter
of chance. The very urgent appeal "come back" directed by the
chorus (the daughters of Jerusalem) to the young woman is immediately followed by a rather enigmatic question by the young
man to this same chorus: "What are you looking at in the Shulamite as in a dance of two camps?" The answer to this question
seems to be given immediately by the young man himself who
undertakes the praise of his loved one in describing her from foot
to head. This *wasf* constitutes the main part of the ninth poem,
with 7:1 serving as its rhetorical introduction. But in what way
can this section be connected to 6:11–12?

The answer, it seems to me, would be that the poet is calling
to mind the outstanding event which marked the beginning of
David's reign, namely, the transfer of the Ark to Jerusalem.[10] The
very name *šûlammît* already brings to mind, as has often been
noted, the name of the beautiful Abishag of Shunem, who became the companion of David toward the end of his life. But another more important allusion is one already suggested by D.
Buzy: "Since Amminadab in this passage is associated with a sa-

cred cart, is this not sufficient reason to mention them together in the Song?" " . . . Because the sacred cart carried the Ark, is this not a motive for comparing the bride poetically to the cart carrying the beloved spouse?" Buzy translates: "My love made me the chariot of Aminadab." However, according to Buzy, it is the husband and not the bride who speaks in verses 11 and 12.[11] On the contrary, it is the bride according to the Septuagint which even adds to the end of verse 11 the final words of 7:13: "There I will give you my breast (in Hebrew: my caresses)." In actual fact, it is definitely the young woman who resumes the end of 6:11 in 7:13; it is she then who speaks in 6:11 and also in 6:12. The verbs in the perfect tense, *yrdty*, "I went down" and *yd'ty*, "I knew" correspond and have the same subject, namely, the young woman.

A. Touassi had indicated the sense of this passage well enough when he paraphrased it this way: "The desire of my heart made me think of myself as the royal cart on which my divine spouse was seated."[12] The Ark can in fact be compared to a divine throne.[13] As for the narratives about the transfer of the Ark in the books of Samuel, namely, 1 Samuel 6:7 and 2 Samuel 6:3, they mention each time a new chariot; so several chariots would have been necessary to transport the Ark;[14] hence the plural *markebôt* in Song 6:12 which must then be translated:

I knew not my heart:
it made of me the chariots of Ammi-nadab.

In Song 6:12, the reading Ammi-nadab (*ndb* without a yod) is found in twenty manuscripts, as well as in the Septuagint and the Vulgate. In the books of Samuel, the Septuagint has the reading Aminadab in place of the Hebrew Abinadab, with the exception of 3 Kings 4:11 where the Codex Alexandrinus reads Abinadab. The two names can easily be confused. In Numbers

10:14, the Codex Ambrosianus reads Abinadab instead of the Hebrew Amminadab. A brother of David was named Abinadab (1 Sam. 16:8; 17:13; 1 Chron. 2:13), while an officer of David was named Amminadab according to 1 Chronicles 15:10–11.[15] In Esther 2:7, the Greek adds the name of Aminadab, the uncle of Mordecai. We may note also that in Song 7:2, the Septuagint has transcribed *nadab* as in 6:12 in place of the Hebrew *nādîb*.

If *'ammî-nādîb* of Song 6:12 can bring to mind the story of Abinadab, at whose home in Kiriath-Jearim the Ark remained (1 Sam. 7:1), the word *nādîb*, repeated in Song 7:2, takes on great significance in the light of the book of Chronicles. As a matter of fact, the Chronicler has a special fondness for the verb *nādab* and its derivatives, especially the *hithpael* form "to commit oneself,"[16] to emphasize the noble, generous, spontaneous character of the appointment to the service of YHWH in the temple of Jerusalem, the permanent residence of the Ark, the place of the invisible presence of God (the *Shekinah*) in the midst of his people Israel. Rereading 1 Chronicles 29, the beautiful prayer pronounced by David, placed a few lines before the narrative of the accession of his son Solomon, one is struck by the numerous contacts with the Song of Songs.

In verses 5–6, the leaders of the people *commit themselves* to donate great treasures to the service of God. And the text continues: "[9] The people (*'ām*) rejoiced at that to which they had *committed themselves*, for it was with a heart (*lēb*) not divided (*šālēm*)[17] that they had *committed themselves* to YHWH; King David himself was filled with joy." And in his benediction, David cried out: "[14] Who am I and what is my people (*'ammî*) to have sufficient means to *commit ourselves* in this way?" And he continued: "[17] I know (*yāda'tî*), my God, that you examine the heart (*lēbāb*) and that you are pleased (*tirseh*) with integrity; for me, it is with an upright heart (*lebābî*) that I have *committed myself* to all this, and at this moment I have watched with joy your people (*'ammēkā*) here present *commit themselves* to you. [18] YHWH, God of Abraham, Isaac and Israel our ancestors, watch over this forever, shape the inclination of the heart (*lebab*) of your people ('*ammekā*) and guide their heart (*lĕbābām*)."

In addition to the repetition of the verb *ndb*, we should note in this text the words: "I know," "my people," and even "the heart," a synonym of *nefeš* of Song 6:12. The terminology is similar to Song 6:12 and helps us understand better how the name of Abinadab has been altered to Amminadib. While referring to the famous episode of the transfer of the Ark, the poet had in mind the sentiments of the daughter of Zion preparing herself to greet her "fiancé," the new Solomon, the King-Messiah of Zion.

It is for the same purpose that the poet modifies slightly the name of the beautiful Abishag the "Shulamite"[18] by making up the name "*šûlammît*": David did not "know" Abishag; she was intended for a greater "king," the one whom God has "chosen" to be a son and for whom he will be a "father" (1 Chron. 28:5–6, 10; 29:1), the one who will sit on the royal throne of YHWH. Codex Vaticanus transcribes *šûlammît: soumaneitis* and *soumaneitidi*.[19] The very name of the village of Shunem has become Sulem today. It is the Beit Sulamiye of Guerin; medieval Solem was a benefice of Mount Thabor. Thus the consonants *l*, *m* and *n* can easily be interchanged among themselves. The form *šûlammît*, a past participle, is analogous to '*ukkāl* (Ex. 3:2), *yûllād* (Jgs. 13:8).[20] It means "the woman who brings peace," as Aquila and Quinta clearly understood by translating *eireneuousa*. So this name *šûlammît* corresponds in the Song to the name of *šēlōmōh*, Solomon; both are derived from the same root *šlm*,[21] to be whole, upright, complete, from which is derived "to be at peace." These two names correspond to the French names Irénée and Irène or the English name Irene. According to 1 Samuel 7:1 and 14 there was peace in Israel after the great victory over the Philistines and the transfer of the Ark to the house of Abinadab.

Names derived from the root *šlm* are very numerous in the Persian period, after the return from Exile.[22] We may mention especially *mešullām*, "he who is restored, or rehabilitated," a name attributed in Isaiah 42:19 to a reconciled Israel; the sinful and idolatrous people has disappeared and in its place appears the new Israel, reestablished in a covenant of peace (Is. 53:5; 54:10). The name *Mešullām* was given to the child who replaced an older child who died prematurely.[23] In the name *Šûlammît*, it is rather the aspect of peace which is emphasized, just as in the name *Šēlōmōh*, the Peaceful.

Chapter 9 of the first book of Chronicles contains many names of Levites, formed from the root *šlm*: Meshullam (four times), Shallum (four times), Meshillemith (once), Meshelemiah (once). In this same chapter, mention is made in verses 29–30 of wine, oil, incense, perfumes, and aromatic mixtures. There they speak too of valiant heroes (v. 13), one thousand seven hundred and sixty of them; there are only sixty in Song 3:7, but the numerical contact should be noted. There is talk also of Levites who "spend the night" in the precincts of the house of God. All this brings to mind to some extent Song 3:7–8. Finally, the Chronicler calls Jerusalem in verse 19 the *camp* of YHWH; there the Tent or House of God was installed (vv. 23, 26–27). This mention of the camp in connection with Jerusalem is to be kept in mind.

In fact, in Chronicles Jerusalem is assimilated to the Israelite camp of the time of the Exodus. The return from Babylon is compared in the second part of the book of Isaiah, and elsewhere as well, to the coming out of Egypt seven centuries earlier. Zion has become the second Sinai from which law goes out (Is. 2:3; Mic. 4:2; cf. Ps. 68:18). This priestly ideology is reflected in the expression "Jerusalem, camp of YHWH," the dwelling place of his Glory. In 1 Chron. 12:23, it is stated that the camp of David had become as large as a "camp of God," a form of superlative equivalent to gigantic or immense. This section is just before the

account of the decision to transfer the Ark to Jerusalem (13:3ff).
We meet the phrase "camp of God" again under the form "camp
of YHWH" in 1 Chron. 9:19 and 2 Chron. 31:2 (cf. Zech. 9:8;
Deut. 23:15; Jos. 6:23).

This brings us back to Song 7:1 which speaks of a dance of
two camps. The Hebrew word *maḥănāyim* is in the dual form, but
the Greek versions and the Vulgate have a plural, "camps." The
alliteration has often been emphasized, and attempts have been
made in various ways to give a description of this dance.[24] Some
have thought of a dance and a counter-dance, of the goings and
comings of two groups of singers and dancers.[25] Others are re-
minded of the sabre dance that the new bride performs, the eve-
ning of her wedding, in Syria, in the Djebel Hauran. However,
A. Robert prefers to compare it with a famous episode in the Jacob story: Genesis 32.

The patriarch's clan had become so numerous that it was
necessary to divide it into *two* camps, *maḥănôth* (v. 11).[26] But, in
Song 6:4, shortly before the text that concerns us, the poet had
mentioned Tirzah (and not Samaria!) with Jerusalem, the *two*
capitals in Israel and Judah after the death of Solomon, severed
by the schism of the ten tribes since the reigns of Jeroboam I and
Rehoboam, son of Solomon. Their reconciliation and reunification were often envisaged and hoped for in the period of the Second Temple. Numerous texts witness to this.[27] The Chronicler
insists on it a great deal, especially in the account of King Hezekiah's Passover.[28] It is possible that Psalm 68:28 also makes an
allusion to it: this verse mentions Judah and Benjamin, Zebulon
and Naphtali.[29]

This theme of reunification is connected to the theme of *return*.[30] Genesis 32:10 already brings to mind the divine command:
"Go back to your native land," found precisely before the mention of the "two camps." 2 Chronicles 30:6 quotes the words of
King Hezekiah's courtiers: "Israelites, return to YHWH." This

deuteronomic formula appears in 1 Samuel 7:3; Samuel says to Israel: "Return to YHWH with all your heart," right after a passage which describes the installation of the Ark at Kiriath-jearim. In a postexilic addition to the book of Jeremiah in which there is also question of the Ark of the covenant and its disappearance (3:16), YHWH repeats several times the exhortation "Come back," addressed to Israel (vv. 12, 14), after having established that neither Israel nor Judah had yet "come back" to him (vv. 7, 10). Once again, the *two* kingdoms of the North and the South are mentioned together. The conclusion of this oracle announces that the house of Judah will join the house of Israel (v. 18): this is the theme developed by the Chronicler in chapter 30, referred to above.

Now the fourfold "Come back" of Song 7:1, addressed to the Shulamite, could certainly be explained from such a perspective, just like the dance of two camps.[31] In fact, the transfer of the Ark by David and its "return" to Zion were accompanied by dances of the whole house of Israel and her king, David. Therefore, it is amid dances and joyful songs that the "return" of the Virgin of Israel to the heights of Zion will take place (Jer. 31:4, 13): "Come home, Virgin of Israel, come home to these towns of yours" (Jer. 31:21). In this way, a transposition is made of the primitive meaning in which the fourfold *šwby* could have referred to the rotation of the dancer, her whirling.[32]

In Song 7:1, the fourfold entreaty "Come back" can remind us of the return of the exiles of Judah from the four quarters of the world, a theme well attested in other texts.[33] Already, the Yahwist had described in a summary way the symbolic taking of the Promised Land, starting from the four points of the compass.[34] And in Numbers 10:36, Moses would say when the Ark halted: "Come back, Lord! Countless are the thousands of Israel."[35]

Without any emending of the received text, we can explain

Song 6:12–7:1 then by referring to the story of David: his transfer of the Ark to Zion and the episode of Abishag of Shunem.
The poet will have intentionally changed the names *'Ăbînādāb*
and *Šûnammît* to indicate clearly his intention of suggesting a
messianic reading. The daughter of Zion has indeed become a
"theophoric" people. YHWH has established in her the place of
his dwelling and of his repose. She has pledged herself to serve
him in Zion, *there* where he dwells.[36] The transfer of the Ark
in the time of David prefigures the renewal of worship, beginning in 515, by the Jews repatriated to Judah at the time of Zerubbabel. As in the time of David and Solomon, the people of
Israel will then recover a certain unity, and Jerusalem, under
Nehemiah, will become once more a beautiful city, whose
splendor is praised in many poetical texts (Is. 60 and 62; Ps.
45:12; 48:3; 50:2; etc.). Gathered together from the four quarters of the world, her inhabitants will receive the gift of peace
in the midst of merrymaking and joyful dancing (Jer. 31:4;
Zech. 8:12).

It is true that the verb *šûb* can also be understood in the
sense of "to be converted"; hence in Ezekiel 33:11 there is repeated twice: "Return, return (from your evil conduct . . .
House of Israel)." The Midrash Rabba on the Song of Songs,
in referring to Song 7:1, quotes Isaiah 66:12: "I am going to
send peace toward her like a river": it is in being converted that
Israel and each Israelite in particular will become a "peacemaker" for the whole world.[37] God therefore invites unfaithful
Israel to repent by calling her *šûlammît*, for Israel is the people
who is to establish "peace" between God and the world.[38] In
this midrashic interpretation, it is question of a new development which goes beyond the immediate sense of Song 7:1 interpreted in the light of the historical books of Samuel, Kings
and Chronicles.

✳

✳   ✳

---

¹ This is the opinion of O. LORETZ, *Studien zur althebraischen Poesie* (AOAT 14/1, 1971), p. 41; similarly J. ANGÉNIEUX, *ETL* 44 (1968), p. 128.

² Thus L. KRINETZKI, *Bib* 52 (1971), p. 188. I proposed an analogous explanation for Ps. 71:15: "Notules sur les Psaumes," *Alttestamentliche Studien F. Nötscher* . . . (BBB I, 1950), pp. 277–80. SHALOM PAUL compares it to the Akkadian phrase *ramānšu la īde*, "he does not know himself" ("An Unrecognized Medical Idiom in Canticles 6,12 and Job 9,21," *Bib* 59 (1978), pp. 545–46).

³ *Op. cit.*, pp. 245, 248; the *TOB* uses this conjecture.

⁴ *A Study of the Language of Love* . . . , 1978, p. 46.

⁵ "Les suffixes verbaux non accusatifs dans le sémitique nord," *Bib* 45 (1964), p. 244; quoted by POPE, p. 587.

⁶ *Ruth. Das Hohelied*, 1965, p. 191.

⁷ *Op. cit.*, p. 552 and fig. 11. In the "lyrical description" published by J. NOUGAYROL (*Ugaritica* 5, 1968, p. 365) the "mother" is identified among other things with a chariot of juniper, a litter of palm.

⁸ *The New English Bible*, 1970, p. 805 (an emended Hebrew text).

⁹ Pss. 39:9; 102:2; 147:14.

¹⁰ See R. TOURNAY, "Les chariots d'Aminadab (Cant. VI, 12): Israël, peuple théophore," *VT* 9 (1959), pp. 288–309.

¹¹ *Le Cantiques des Cantiques* (La Sainte Bible VI, 1946), Paris, pp. 346–47.

¹² *Le Cantique des Cantiques de Salomon*, Abbeville, 1919, p. 65.

¹³ Cf. R. de VAUX, "Les chérubins et l'arche d'alliance, les sphinx

gardiens et les trônes divins dans l'ancien Orient," *Bible et Orient*," 1967, pp. 231–59; F. LANGLAMET, "Les récits de l'institution de la royauté (1 Sam. VII–XII)," *RB* 77 (1970), p. 182.

14 On the transportation of statues of conquered deities, cf. H. D. PREUSS, *Verspottung fremder Religionem im A.T.*, (BWANT 5, 12/92, 1970), Stuttgart, pp. 215–24; M. COGAN, *Imperialism and Religion*, 1974, pp. 22–41. The *merkābâ* ("chariot"; the word is from 1 Chron. 28:18) of Ezekiel (chap. 1 and 10; cf. Sirach 49:8) carries the Glory of YHWH; it is well known that this theme gives rise to much speculation in the Midrashes and in Jewish Kabbala.

15 At least three Ammonite kings were named Amminadab. This name is also found on seals (cf. R. HESTRIN and MICHAL DAYAGI-MENDELS, *Inscribed Seals*, Israel Museum, Jerusalem, 1979, p. 129).

16 1 Chron. 28:21; 2 Chron. 17:16; 29:31; 31:14; 35:8; cf. Ezra 1:46; 2:68; 3:5; 8:28; Neh. 9:2; Ps. 110:3 (Hebrew): "Your people is generosity itself (spontaneously)": this reading would come from a rereading in Levitical circles and may be compared with 1 Macc. 2:42 and to the Rule of the Qumran Community (1:7; etc.) which speaks of "volunteers of the Torah" (cf. F.-M. ABEL and J. STARCKY, *Les livres des Maccabées*, 3rd ed., 1961, p. 99, note c).

17 The phrase is found again in v. 19; cf. also 2 Kgs. 2:3; Is. 38:3; 1 Chron. 12:38; 28:9; 29:9,19; 2 Chron. 15:17; 19:9; 25:2. But the phrase "with the whole heart" occurs very frequently.

18 1 Kgs. 2:17ff.; cf. 1 Sam. 28:4; 2 Kgs. 4:8,25. In regard to Shunem, cf. F.-M. ABEL, *Géographie de la Palestine*, II, 1938, p. 470.

19 As in 3 Kgs. 1:15 and 4 Kgs. 4:12.

20 After the vowel *a* there is a spontaneous doubling of the consonant *m* (JOÜON, n. 18f, 58b).

21 Cf. H. H. SCHMID, *Šalom: Frieden im Alten Orient und im Alten Testament* (Stuttgarter Bibelstudien 51), 1971.

22 Cf. M. NOTH, *Israelitische Personennamen*, p. 165. M. Dotan has found the name *šlmy* on a jar from Azor (*Atiqot* 3, 1961, p. 183).

23 Cf. R. TOURNAY, *RB* 75 (1968), p. 592.

24 Cf. A. STRUS, *Nomen-Omen* (AnBib 80, 1978), Rome, p. 74.

25 In regard to dances for women, cf. O. LORETZ, *Studien zur althebräischen Poesie. I. Das althebräische Liebeslied*, pp. 42–43. On responsorial or alternating singing in Israel, cf. R. TOURNAY, *RB* 78 (1971), p. 24, notes 31–32; and already among the Sumerians, cf. J. KRECHER, *Sumerische Kultlyrik*, 1966, pp. 42–43.

26 Cf. A. de PURY, *Promesse divine et légende cultuelle dans le cycle de Jacob*, 1975, p. 98. David will cross over to Mahanaim (2 Sam. 2:8; 17:24). In regard to this site, cf. K. O. SCHUNCK, "Erwägungen zur Geschichte und Bedeutung von Mahanaim," *ZDPV* 113 (1963), pp. 34–40.

27 Jer. 3:18; 23:16; 31:6; 33:24; 50:4,33; 51:5; Ez. 37:5ff.; Hos. 2:2; Mic. 2:12; Zech. 9:13; 10:6; Ps. 80; etc.

28 2 Chron. 30:5,10,18,25; 31:1; cf., before that, 1 Chron. 9:3. See H. G. M. WILLIAMSON, *Israel in the Book of Chronicles*, 1977, pp. 119–30.

29 Cf. R. TOURNAY *et al.*, *Les Psaumes* (BdJ), 3rd ed., p. 293, note p.

30 In regard to the verb *šûb*, "come back," "be converted," etc., cf. W. L. HOLLADAY, *The Root Šûbh in the Old Testament with Particular Reference to its Usages in Covenantal Contexts*, Leiden, 1958.

31 It has been suggested that *šûb* be given the meaning "to dance," following a Qumran text (4QS, 1, 40, 4 and 7:

angelic liturgy: rule for singing for the Sabbath holocaust). Cf. H.-J. FABRY, *Die Wurzel šûb in der Qumran-Literatur* (BBB 46), 1975, p. 254.

³² Cf. M. I. GRUBER, "Ten Dance-Derived Expressions in the Hebrew Bible," *Bib* 62 (1981), pp. 343–44.

³³ Is. 43:5–6; Zech. 2:10; 6:5; Ps. 107:3; cf. Is. 11:12.

³⁴ Cf. A. de PURY, *op. cit.*, 1975, pp. 179–80 (Gen. 13:14; 28:14; Deut. 3:27).

³⁵ The text is uncertain and has been emended in various ways. The inverted *nuns* indicate that the text has been tampered with. Cf. B. A. LEVINE, "More on the Inverted Nuns of Num. 10:35–36," *JBL* 95 (1976), pp. 122–25.

³⁶ A Marian application could be considered in the perspective of the mystery of the Visitation. The Virgin Mary "carries" the Messiah expected by Israel and the one come to save all people. Following E. BURROWS (*The Gospel of the Infancy*, 1940, p. 47), R. LAURENTIN has shown that the Visitation narrative makes use of the typology of the Ark of the Covenant and directs us back to the story of the transfer of the ark by David (*Structure de Luc I–II*, pp. 79ff., 118, 151).

³⁷ Cf. *The Midrash*, IX, *Song of Songs*, 3rd ed., 1961 (The Soncino Press, London), p. 275. See above, p. 79.

³⁸ Cf. J. Dupont, *Les Béatitudes*, III (Études Bibliques), 1973, p. 640, note 3.

Chapter Eight

THE DAVIDIC-SOLOMONIC MESSIAH

*T*he books of Chronicles reserve a privileged place for Kings David and Solomon, sometimes mentioned side by side (2 Chron. 7:11; 8:14; 11:17; 30:26; cf. Neh. 12:45). The shadows over their reigns are carefully passed over in silence. David is presented as the founder of Temple worship, and Solomon as the builder of the Temple. Levitical worship and the organization of the sanctuary are at the heart of the narrative. The prophecy of Nathan, made to David, assumes a fundamental importance, for it announces that the promise in regard to Davidic descent will be realized first in one of his sons, namely, Solomon; the Chronicler insists very much on the divine choice. Acting wisely is the only possibility seen for Solomon, contrary to what was envisaged in 2 Samuel 7:14: "If he does wrong, I will punish him with a rod such as men use. . . . " Solomon will fully realize then the program contained in his name; he will bring peace and tranquility to Israel (1 Chron. 22:9); this peace will be the fruit of justice (Is. 32:17; Zech. 9:9–10). Here we meet up with the same picture presented to us by the author of Psalm 72, according to its title a psalm to be attributed to Solomon.

It is later on, in the Hellenistic period, that the sages of Israel will reflect on the present and past misfortunes of Israel, and above all, on the schism of the ten tribes; they will make Solomon responsible for this division from which Israel will never recover. So Qoheleth refers to Rehoboam, the fool, successor of a sage (2:18–19) and Sirach recalls the failings of Solomon (47:19–21; cf. Neh. 13:26). As for David, later generations preserve the memory of him as the ancestor of the Messiah, "son of David," "branch of David" (Jer. 23:5; 33:15). This last phrase is found in the Qumran texts.[1] In regard to the phrase "my servant David," after the Exile it acquired a distinctly Messianic coloring, as seen for example in Psalms 89 and 132.[2]

In contrast to the explicit allusions to Solomon, the Song of Songs mentions David only once in regard to the "tower of David" (*dwyd*, 4:4). Should we proceed no further and just admit that there is no other reference, even an implicit one, to the father of Solomon? I do not think so.

We should note, to start with, that the name David, *dwyd*, is composed of the same consonants as the word *dôdî*, *dwdy*, "my beloved." In 1:13–14 the young woman uses this epithet twice, as if to stress it, of the one that her heart loves (1:17); she adds that her beloved is a King as she has already stated in 1:4 and 12. Let us examine all the occurrences of *dwd* in the Song. We find *dôdî*, "my beloved" twenty-six times, and "your beloved" the four times when the chorus questions the young woman (5:9; 6:1). In 5:9, *dôd* is used twice without a pronominal suffix; in 8:5, we find "her beloved" in a question asked by the chorus. In all, *dôd* is mentioned thirty-three times. Each time the young woman speaks, she says "my beloved." The only description that she gives of her beloved—in his absence, it should be noted—is preceded (5:8–10) and followed (5:16 and 6:1–3) each time by six mentions of the word *dôd*. That provides a symmetrical framework which must be intentional.

In the books of Samuel and Kings (except for 1 Kgs. 3:14 and 11:4), the name of David is written *dwd* without the *yod*, exactly like *dôd*; it is the same in the book of Psalms. The *yod*, *mater lectionis*, appears in the postexilic books: Ezra, Nehemiah, Chronicles, Zechariah, as well as the additions in Amos 9:11 and Ezekiel 34:23; the same is the case in the Qumran texts. We should note too that the word *dôd* is never used in the feminine in the Song to refer to the young woman.[3] She is called *ra'yātî*, "my love," eight times, and *kallâ*, fiancée, six times. The plural *dôdîm*, "dear ones" (5:1), used of people,[4] is unique in the Song. It is parallel then to *rē'îm*, "friends," and has been interpreted in varying ways. Does it refer to marriage attendants, to friends of the young couple? A little farther on (5:16), there is the same parallelism between "my beloved" and "my loved one," but these words refer to the young man and the young woman. With Lys, Gerleman, etc., we may consider that, in 5:1, it only refers to the two lovers. Indeed, this is the simplest solution. This passage is also compared to 1 Kings 4:20: in the time of Solomon, they ate, they drank, they were happy (cf. 2 Sam. 11:11 and Eccles. 3:12–13).

The abstract plural *dōdîm*, meaning "caresses,"[5] is found in the prologue (1:2–4), 4:10, and in the conclusion (7:13). The versions read it as *dadîm*, "breasts," as in Proverbs 5:19 (Massoretic text). But the abstract plural is found in Proverbs 7:18 where it means "pleasure," and in Ezekiel 16:8 and 23:17 where it means "love."

If the names of Solomon and of Jerusalem are found associated several times in the Song: namely, at the beginning (1:1,3), at the end (8:4,11,12) and in the description of the wedding procession (3:5,7,9–11), it is the same for *dôdî* and Jerusalem in 2:7,8; 8:4,5, and especially in the verses surrounding the description of the young man: 5:8ff.,16; 6:1–3. Perhaps there is a clue here that suggests thinking of David when *dôd* is mentioned. The very name David is the *qātîl* form of the root *dwd*, that is to say, "beloved, loved" (by his parents, by Israel, especially by YHWH). Now, the title *yĕdîdyâ* given to Solomon by the prophet Nathan (2 Sam. 12:25; cf. Sir. 47:18 Hebr.) has the same meaning "beloved of YHWH"; *yādîd* is also a *qātîl* form (like *nāgîd*, *nāśî*, *māšîaḥ*, etc.), and is considered a passive participle of the root *ydd*, a variant of the root *dwd*, with both being derived from the onomatopoeic *dad*.[6] These two words are found associated at the beginning of the song of the vineyard, in Isaiah 5:1: the well-beloved, the fiancé, is going to sing about and against his fiancée. . . .[7]

It is true that some have wanted to see in the *dôd* of the Song a replica of Tammuz, the lover of women (cf. Ez. 8:14). There is no reason to accept this hypothesis, a corollary of the mythological interpretation of the Song of Songs, now long outmoded. However, it is not unreasonable to suppose some Egyptian influence here, since the names of David and Jedidiah can be compared to many Egyptian names of royalty, formed from the attributive "loved," followed by the name of a deity. In the Song, the *dôd* is solely the "beloved" par excellence, as is indicated by the final words of the young woman, the culmination of the description of her beloved: "Such is my beloved, such is my loved one, daughters of Jerusalem" (5:16).

Solomon and David happen to be associated also by their "heroes." The annalists attribute a great deal of importance to the "heroes of David" (2 Sam. 23:8–39; 1 Chron. 11:10–47; 12:19). But the Song speaks of the shields of "heroes" in connection with the tower of David (4:4) and it had already mentioned the sixty heroes who surrounded King Solomon, with swords at their sides (3:7–8).[8]

We may wonder then whether the poet does not wish to make a more or less implicit allusion to David when he develops the description of the young man (5:10–16). The question comes up as early as the first verse (v. 10) which is translated in many ways:

"My beloved is fresh and ruddy, he stands out among ten thousand."[9]
"My dear one is light and ruddy, he is more conspicuous than ten thousand."[10]

"My dear one, clear and ruddy, conspicuous above a myriad."[11]
"My lover is radiant and ruddy; he stands out among thousands."[12]
"My beloved is fair and ruddy, a paragon among ten thousand."[13]
"My love is radiant and ruddy, conspicuous above a myriad."[14]

In this passage, the epithet '*ādôm*, red, much like Edom, the "red one" (Gen. 25:25), reminds us of the epithet '*admônî* used to refer to the young David in 1 Samuel 16:12 and 17:42.[15] The Versions translate it "ruddy." Sometimes the translation "fair complexion" is suggested, to emphasize the youthfulness of David, an adolescent, despised for that reason by the Philistines (1 Sam. 17:42).[16] Moreover, the mention of "ten thousand" cannot help but recall several acclamations used in greeting King David. The troops who accompanied him declare: "You are like ten thousand of us" (2 Sam. 18:3).[17] The women, not to be outdone, repeat the ovation given the victorious David by crying out: "Saul has killed his thousands and David his tens of thousands" (1 Sam. 18:7; 21:12; 29:5). The echo of this reaches as far as Sirach, in the Hebrew text: "Hence the women sang for him and named him Ten Thousand" (47:6); the Greek text is similar, but lengthier: "Hence they gave him credit for ten thousand and praised him while they blessed the Lord by offering him a crown of glory."

However, in the description of the young man that follows (Song 5:11–16) there seems to be no allusion, even in passing, to the person of King David. Taking advantage of a suggestion he had received, A. Robert tried to see in this section a series of allusions to the Jerusalem Temple. The head of the spouse, of gold, would be compared to the Holy of Holies. The shields would bring to mind the palms and flowers carved on the cedar panelling and on the folding doors of the Holy Place (1 Kgs. 6:18,29,32,33). The blackness of the raven suggests the darkness of the Holy of Holies without any windows. Verses 12–13 recall the basin of lustral water, the bronze Sea where the priests purified themselves and whose edge (literally: lip) resembled the lip of a cup, or was like a fleur-de-lis (1 Kgs. 7:26). The hands bring to mind the two massive columns (1 Kgs. 7:15–22); and the belly, the vestibule of the sanctuary. The legs would be the pedestals of silver or bronze and the colonnades (cf. Sirach 26:18). Finally, the cedars of Lebanon (v. 15) were abundantly used in the building of the Temple. Lebanon is mentioned seven times elsewhere in the Song. In the Targums and the rabbinic literature, the word Lebanon came to be used to refer to the Temple of Jerusalem. This is already the case in the *Pesher* (commentary) on Habakkuk, discovered in Cave One at Qumran.[18]

    A. Robert's interpretation has been much criticized. G. Gerleman has proposed another explanation, starting with Egyptian statuary.[19] Egyptian statues were in fact painted in dark ochre for men, in light ochre for women. The Hebrew phrase *ṣaḥ wě'ādôm* could mean "light ochre." Other details in the description of the young man could no doubt be understood in the same way. We would have here, once again, an indication of Egyptian influence on the Song. But this is far from excluding every specifically biblical connection, as, for example, allusion to the beauty of David, ancestor of the King-Messiah, the fairest of human beings (Ps. 45:3),[20] and, why not too, allusion to the Temple, the paragon of beauty. Metaphors and symbols have their own logic, namely, that of poetry. The young woman could have described her beloved as a divine statue, by applying to him elements from a variety of sources, even mythological ones, along with allusions to David and to the Temple. Just as in Proverbs 3:13ff; 8:10ff; Sirach 50:6ff, comparisons follow and mutually reinforce one another; both Semitic and Egyptian literatures have a liking for juxtaposed images.[21]

David is the King-Shepherd par excellence. He was a shepherd "following the sheep" when Samuel came looking for him to make him leader of Israel.[22] The conclusion of Psalm 78 (verses 70–72) calls to mind David, the wise shepherd of unblemished heart. Psalm 151 (Septuagint) speaks of David the shepherd.[23] Ezekiel announces the coming of an ideal shepherd, "my servant David," who will be prince over Israel.[24] Micah speaks of the shepherding role of the Messiah to come.[25]

Now, the theme of the shepherd and the flock comes up from the beginning of the Song (1:7–8). The young woman asks the one she loves where he leads the *flock* to pasture and where he will take them to rest at noon. She no longer wishes to wander[26] near the flocks of his friends. The chorus—the daughters of Jerusalem mentioned in verse 5—tell her to follow the tracks of the flock and take her young goats to graze near the shelters of the shepherds. This shepherd theme also concludes the formula of mutual belonging: "My beloved is mine and I am his; he is a *shepherd* among the lilies" (2:16; 6:3).[27] We have already emphasized (p. 93) the ambiguity of this phrase; the participle *rō'eh* can mean either "to pasture and to feed himself " (the meaning found in the Vulgate), or "to take to feed" (the meaning found in the Septuagint). Commentators continue to be puzzled here; they often refer to scenes of sheep-folds and flocks, as well as the picking of lotuses, themes often depicted on bas-reliefs in Egypt.[28] Once again, the poet would be inspired by Egypt, without thinking of any king-shepherd or more precisely of David, but when the young woman puts *dwdy*, "my beloved" and *r'y*, "my loved one" (5:16) in parallelism, it may be asked whether a "double entendre" is not possible, both for *r'y* which could be understood as "my shepherd" as well as for *dwd* which could refer to David: these words are written with the same consonants, and only the vowel-pointing can differentiate between them.[29]

David and his son Solomon are both associated with a common imagery, that of the vine-grower. Already the oracle of Jacob on Judah (Genesis 49:10ff.), the tribe from which the heir of David will come, sees in this heir a vine-grower who tethers his donkey to the vine and to its stock the foal of his she-donkey, and who washes his clothes in wine and his robes in the blood (*dam*) of the grapes. In Isaiah 63:2–3 this imagery is applied to God himself, avenger of his people at the expense of the pagans: "Why are your garments red (*'ādōm*), and your clothes like someone treading the winepress?—'I have trodden the winepress alone . . . their juice (that of the pagans) squirted over my garments and all my clothes are stained.' " The Targumists apply these texts directly to the Messiah whose beauty they emphasize at the same time: "How handsome he is, the King Messiah who should arise from among those who are of the house of Judah! He ties a loincloth around his waist and sets out for combat against his enemies, and he kills the kings with the leaders. He reddens the mountains with the blood of those killed and whitens the hills with the fat of their warriors. His garments are soaked in the blood and he looks like a treader of grapes."[30]

In the Song, the vineyard (1:6,14; 2:13,15; 6:11; 7:9,13), the grapes (7:9) and the wine (1:2,4; 3:10; 4:10–5:1; 7:10; 8:2) occupy a large place. According to 8:11, Solomon had a vineyard at Baal-Hamon (see p. 39). The attendants had to run it and shared in the crop of grapes valued at an enormous sum, a thousand pieces of silver. This number has been compared to the thousand women, wives and concubines (1 Kings 11:3) of the historical Solomon. Here, the image of the vine, a traditional figure of Israel, can be transposed in a Messianic perspective. For the new Solomon the daughter of Zion alone counts; she is fully at his disposal. But such an interpretation remains hypothetical, for this passage has not yet received a satisfactory explanation.

One final consideration will perhaps produce a smile. The word *dôd* with or without a suffix occurs thirty-three times in the Song. Now David reigned thirty-three years at Jerusalem (1 Kings 2:11; 1 Chronicles 29:27). Is this a pure coincidence?

The final mention of *dôd* is found in the last verse of the book-let, 8:14: "Flee,[31] my beloved, and be like the gazelle or the young fawn on the mountains of spices." We know that this verse repeats 2:17, but with variants. Already 8:13 repeats some words of 2:14: "Make me hear your voice." These final verses could have been added by a final redactor. But, in 8:11–12, Solomon is mentioned twice, which makes seven mentions in all of his name in the whole Song. The same redactor could have tried to obtain thirty-three mentions of the word *dôd*, an equivalent of David.

Be that as it may, a messianic reading of the Song is justified in discovering, beside the personage of Solomon, that of his father, David too.[32] Both together form in Jewish tradition the ideal complete type of the King-Messiah. Both together are readily idealized in the Book of Chronicles; it could be the same in the Song. Just as the woman is faithful to the friend of her younger days and does not forget the covenant of her God (Proverbs 2:17), the daughter of Zion does not fail to discover through the descriptions in the Song the model of the King-Messiah, a new David. The Song in this way joins up with the book of Chronicles which considers the reign of David as the type of the theocratic kingdom which heralds the ideal epoch, that of Solomon the Peacemaker.[33] We may note that Psalms 2 and 110 present the messianic king as a warrior chieftain, a combatant who crushes his enemies, a new David. Psalms 45, 72 and 101 present this king instead as a new Solomon.

＊

＊　　＊

[1] Cf. 4Q Flor. 11 and Patriarchal Blessings I, 3 (CARMIGNAC-COTHENET-LIGNÉE, *Les textes de Qumran*, II, 1963, pp. 282, 287).

[2] Cf. 2 Sam. 7:13; 1 Kgs. 1:31; Ps. 89:5; etc. A. KAPELRUD made a comparison with the Ugaritic phrase *mlk 'lm* applied to the God Rpu: "The Ugaritic text RS 24.252 and King David," *Journal of Northwest Semitic Languages* 3 (1974), p. 39. This healing god is very probably identical to the god El; cf. CAQUOT-SZNYCER-HERDNER, *Textes Ougaritiques* (LAPO 7 1974), p. 61, note 1. On David as a messianic figure, cf. J. GARCIA TRAPIELLO, "Influjo de la dinastía davídica en la esperanza messiánica," *La Esperanza en la Biblia*, XXX Semana Biblica Española, Madrid, 1972, pp. 5–20; DENNIS C. DULING, "The Promises to David and their Entrance into Christianity—Nailing Down a Likely Hypothesis," *New Testament Studies* 20 (1974), pp. 55–77; C. BURGER, *Jesus als Davidsohn. Eine traditionsgeschichtlichen Untersuchung* (FRLANT 98, 1970), Göttingen. See also M. GOURGUES, *A la droite de Dieu. Résurrection de Jésus et actualisation du Psaume 110:1 dans le N. T.*, Paris, Gabalda, 1978.

[3] The feminine *dōdâ* means aunt in Ex. 6:20, and the wife of an uncle in Lev. 18:14 and 20:20.

[4] This doubtless refers to two lovers, as D. Lys, G. Gerleman, etc. think.

[5] As LYS (*op. cit.*, p. 63) notes, the translation "caresses" maintains the verbal link with the French "cheri" (Latin *carus*),

which is the translation of *dôd*. (It is more difficult to preserve this link in English, unless we translate *dôd* with some form of the verb "cherish" instead of "beloved.") As seen earlier, *dûdā'îm*, "apples of love," "mandrakes" (7:14; Gen. 30:14–16) is connected with the same root. On the Ugaritic parallels, cf. CAQUOT-SZNYCER-HERDNER, *op. cit.*, pp. 162–64.

6 Cf. H. BLANK, *ZAW* 11 (1891), pp. 127ff; D. N. FREEDMAN, *Textus* 2 (1962), p. 96; A. HOFFMANN, *David, Namensdeutung zur Wesensdeutung* (BWANT 100, 1973), pp. 23–24. For Qumran, cf. E. Y. KUTSCHER, *The Language . . . of the Isaiah Scroll*, Jerusalem, 1959, p. 75. Note Arabic Daoud. There is debate over Sirach 40:20. See J. J. STAMM, *Der Name David* (VTSup 7, 1960), pp. 165–83, reprinted in *Beiträge zum hebräischen und altorientalischen Namengebung*, Fribourg, 1980, pp. 25–43. Cf. Jer. 11:15.

7 Cf. J. T. WILLIS, "The Genre of Isaiah V:1–7," *JBL* 96 (1977), pp. 337–62; J. T. GRAGGY, "The Literary Genre of Isaiah 5:1–7," *UF* 10 (1978), pp. 400–09; H. WILDBERGER, *Jesaja*, p. 164. The mother of King Josiah was called *Yedîdâ* (2 Kgs. 22:1).

8 Nehemiah 3:16 mentions the "house of heroes." According to J. MACDONALD, the name David meant "Champion"; he reviews all the Akkadian texts, especially the Mari Letters wherever there is mention of *dawidum;* in the Mesha Stele, he suggests translating *'r'l dwdh* as "the lion of God (El), his champion": "The Argument that West Semitic DAWIDUM Originally Meant 'Champion,' " *Abr-Nahrain* 17 (1976–77), pp. 52–71. It should be kept in mind that *dawidum* is considered to be an element of Akkadian *dabdum, tapdu*, "defeat."

9 The translation in ROBERT-TOURNAY, pp. 210, 445; also BdJ.

10   The translation of LYS; also *TOB*.

11   The translation of A. CHOURAQUI, *La Bible. Les cinq volumes*, 1975, p. 48.

12   The translation of *The New American Bible. The New International Version* is very similar: "My lover is radiant and ruddy, outstanding among ten thousand." The same is true of the Revised Standard Version: "My beloved is all radiant and ruddy, distinguished among ten thousand"; and *TANAKH, A New Translation of THE HOLY SCRIPTURES* (1985): "My beloved is clear-skinned and ruddy, preeminent among ten thousand."

13   The translation of *The New English Bible*.

14   POPE, p. 8.

15   Cf. R. TOURNAY, *La Cantique des Cantiques. Commentaire abrégé*, 1967, p. 112.

16   We may compare Lam. 4:7: "Once her consecrated ones (literally, Nazirites) were purer than snow, whiter (ṣaḥû) than milk, more ruddy ('ādmû) than coral their bodies." LYS (p. 219) agrees that the young woman could have thought of the features of the handsome King David when speaking of her beloved.

17   Compare Eccles. 7:28: "one man in a thousand I may find."

18   Cf. G. VERMÈS, *Scripture and Tradition in Judaism. Haggadic Studies*, Leiden, 1961, p. 38 (cf. *RB*, 1962, p. 612). CARMIGNAC-COTHENET-LIGNÉE, *op. cit.*, II, 1963, p. 115.

19   "Die Bildsprache des Hohenliedes und die altägyptischen Kunst," *Annual of the Swedish Theological Institute* 1 (1962), pp. 24–30; ID, *Ruth. Das Hohelied*, 1965, pp. 66–71.

20   Is. 33:17 (a postexilic passage) is also applied to the Messiah: "Your eyes will gaze on the king in his beauty." In commenting on Gen. 49:11, the Targum of Pseudo-Jonathan declares: "How beautiful is the King Messiah who must rise up from among those who are of the house of Judah";

cf. p. GRELOT, "L'exégèse messianique d'Isaïe, LXIII, 1–6," *RB* 70 (1963), p. 375.

[21] In Sirach 50:6ff the description of the High Priest Simon, son of Onias, multiplies the comparisons with the sun, the moon, the rainbow, a rose, a lily, the incense tree, a massive golden vessel adorned with every kind of precious stone. The priests around him are compared to the cedars of Lebanon and the trunks of palm trees. See also Sir. 26:18 and Ps. 144:12 for similar comparisons. Cf. b. COUROYER, *RB* 73 (1966), pp. 618–19.

[22] 1 Sam. 13:14; 16:11–12; 17:15,20,28,34; 2 Sam. 7:8. Cf. Ps. 89:28.

[23] The Hebrew text is in 11Q Ps^a; cf. J. CARMIGNAC, "La forme poétique du Psaume 151,1–5," *RevQ* 4 (1963), pp. 379–87; TOB, p. 1441.

[24] Ez. 34:23–24; 37:24; cf. Jer. 33:21; Pss. 18:1; 36:1; 78:70; 89:4ff; 132:10; 144:10.

[25] Cf. b. RENAUD, *La formation du livre de Michée*, 1977, pp. 245–46. On the theme of the king-shepherd, see *JB*, 1985, p. 1449, note a; *TOB*, p. 942, note d.

[26] Reading *to'iyyāh* with Symmachus, Syriac and Vulgate, Targum (cf. Ez. 13:10; Gen. 37:15), instead of the Massoretic text "wrapped, veiled" (cf. Gen. 38:14), a reading adopted by LXX and Aquila. Cf. POPE, pp. 330–31. G. R. DRIVER proposes "delousing" (cf. Jer. 43:12) in his article "Lice in the Old Testament," *PEQ* 106 (1974), pp. 159–60.

[27] See above, p. 62; cf. A. FEUILLET, *RB* 68 (1961), p. 7; LYS, p. 129; POPE, p. 406.

[28] See above, pp. 106f. and p. 112, note 25.

[29] In the time of David and Solomon, a high official had the title "friend of the king," *r'h* (2 Sm. 15:37; 16:16; 1 Kgs. 4:5). The word may perhaps come from Egyptian and have

the same root as *r'h*, "shepherd," and *r'*, "friend" (cf. T. N. D. METTINGER, *Salomonic State Officials*, Lund, 1971, p. 69). At Ugarit, *r'y*, "shepherd" is a title of Hadad according to text 24.259 (*Ugaritica* V, 55, line 3). In the poem of the Rephaim (III R, col. B, line 27), we find *r'h*, "his companion" or "his shepherd" (cf. CAQUOT-SZNYCER-HERDNER, *op. cit.*, p. 477, note p).

[30] Codex Neofiti 1; the text is quoted by P. GRELOT, *"L'exégèse messianique d'Isaïe, LXIII, 1–6,"* *RB* 70 (1963), pp. 375–76. Cf. also Rev. 19:13–15.

[31] David fled to En-Gedi (1 Sam. 24:1) and also to Mahanaim (2 Sam. 17:24); these two place names are mentioned in Song 1:14 and 7:1. Incidentally, this flight of the "beloved" in 8:14 infers nothing; it is merely a departure. Certainly it must be admitted with A.-M. DUBARLE that many such comparisons are "highly conjectural" (*RB* 61 [1954], p. 78, note 4).

[32] According to W. WIFAL, the story of David served as a starting point for Ezekiel, as well as Zech. 9–14 and the New Testament to describe the future of Israel ("David, Prototype of Israel's Future?" *Biblical Theology Bulletin*, Rome, IV, 1974, pp. 94–107). Cf. D. M. GUNN, *The Story of King David. Genre and Interpretation*, JSOT Supplementary Series 6, Sheffield, 1978.

[33] On this typology of the Chronicler, see T. WILLI, *Die Chronik als Auslegung. Untersuchungen zur literarischen Gestaltung der historischen Ueberlieferungs Israels* (FRLANT 106, 1972), Göttingen, p. 104.

Chapter Nine

AN ALLUSION TO KING HIRAM OF TYRE?[1]

*T*he second laudatory description, or *wasf*, which the young man addresses to the one he loves, begins in Song 7:2. The young woman called the "Shulamite" in verse 1 is assumed to be in the act of dancing: "What are you looking at in the Shulamite as in a dance of two camps?" (7:1). In the first *wasf* (4:1ff.), the description begins with the head of the young woman; here, it begins as it should with the feet of the dancer.

The first thing to be noted in verses 1 to 6 of chapter 7 is an accumulation of comparisons. The preposition used in comparisons, *kaph*, "like," is repeated no less than seven times (*kemô* occurs in 2c). There is perhaps also an eighth occurrence in 5b: "Your eyes (like) the pools of Heshbon, by the gate of Bath-Rabbim." But the *kaph* can be understood here without any idea of haplography being present.[2] All these likenesses already direct us toward a symbolic world.

We should note too that stich 5a stands in isolation, without a parallel line: "Your neck is like a tower of ivory." In the first *wasf* (4:4), there was something equivalent, but with a second line: "Your neck is like the tower of David, built in courses."[3] For this reason it has been proposed that a second line be supplied in verse 5, such as *meyussād ʿal-ʾadnê baḥat*, "built on footings of alabaster," like 5:15: "his legs, columns of alabaster, set on pedestals of pure gold." In any case, 7:6c cannot be transferred here, since it is a line whose meaning we must still figure out, and one which does not have a parallel line either: *melek ʾāsûr bārehāṭîm*.

The Massoretic text divides the line before the word *melek*, "king," which is then joined to what follows; the Septuagint also does this:

> On you, your head is like Carmel,
> and the locks of your head are like purple;
> a king is bound in the *rhtym*.

Several versions (Aquila, Symmachus, Peshitta, Vulgate) attach *melek* to the preceding word *'argāmān*, "purple" and translate: "The locks of your head are like royal purple. . . . " So the Vulgate has: "sicut purpura regis, vincta canalibus" ("like the purple of a king, bound in the channels"). Such a division of the verse destroys the structure of the tristich, composed of three stichs of three accents each (ternary rhythm, the most frequent in Hebrew poetry).

The comparison of the head of the young woman with Mount Carmel is the last of a series of comparisons with various localities (in verses 5–6): the pools of Heshbon and the gate of Bath-Rabbim (an unknown place) in Transjordan, then Lebanon and Damascus in Syria: "Your nose is like the tower of Lebanon (perhaps the lofty Hermon), a sentinel facing Damascus." Mount Carmel lends itself very well to a comparison with the head of a young woman. In fact, it is called *roš qadôš*, "holy headland" in the annals of Thut-mose III.[4] In the Egyptian inscription of Uni, the Carmel range is called "the nose of the gazelle."[5] This *răs*, an Arabic word to designate a cape, overlooks, from a height of 552 meters, the Palestinian coast and the plain of Jezreel. Rich vegetation still covers it today. In Isaiah 33:9, this vegetation is compared to the forests of Bashan, and in 35:1 to the glory of Lebanon. Perhaps the author of Song 7:6 wants to recall these texts in order to bring to mind the luxuriant head of hair of the young woman.

Along the coast between Mount Carmel and the region of Tyre they today still collect most beautiful murex, the shell-fish from which purple dye is extracted. A workshop for purple has been discovered at Dor.[6] In the excavations at Tell Keisan, near Acre, a large vat which was used in the manufacture of purple has been found.[7] There is no need then to emend Hebrew *Karmel* to form a word borrowed from Sanscrit, *karmîl*,[8] "crimson," a dye extracted from cochineal.

Already mentioned in Song 3:10, *'argāmān* is red purple, whereas *tĕkēlet* is violet purple. The palanquin of Solomon was made of wood from Lebanon, and its seat was purple (*'argāmān*). Here in 3:10, just as in 7:6, Lebanon and purple are mentioned side by side. Hence in 7:6 the poet compares the locks or tresses, or curls (Hebrew *dallâ⁹*) of the young woman to red purple. What is meant by this? The poet doubtless wishes to emphasize, not the color of the hair or its dye (of henna?), but the brilliant gleam of the hair. We should recall besides that purple dye in olden times was very valuable, even more so than gold or silver, so that *argamannu* in Assyrian designates tribute, just as *arkaman* does in Hittite. Later, purple became the emblem of royal and imperial power; it is for this reason that the versions thought that it would be question here of the royal purple.[10]

Some have wanted to omit this third stich, "a king is bound. . . . " Others have seen here an isolated fragment of a lost poem,[11] or even one of the *melek* comments of the Song.[12] These solutions are too simple and not very respectful of the received text. This third stich is not a doublet as might perhaps be the case for 4:5c, "feeding among the lilies" after "two fawns, twins of a gazelle." In 4:5c, the third stich repeats 2:16b, while 4:6 resumes 2:17. The two passages have been harmonized. It is entirely different in the case of 7:6, for this stich completes the second *wasf*, and it is normal in a lyrical development to finish with an expansion. Furthermore, this stich sets off the mention of the king.

But who is the king being referred to? To find this out, it is necessary to determine the precise meaning of *rehātîm*.

Several explanations have been proposed. We cannot deduce anything from the Targum or the Rabbinic writings which rarely refer to this text.[13] I. Zolli[14] compares this verse with 1:17 where the *kĕtîb, rahîtēnû*, differs from the *qĕrê, rhytnw*, with a *heth* instead of a *hē*. The parallelism with *qōr*, "beam, rafter," suggests that *rhyt* in 1:17 means "ceiling, joists." This is the way the Septuagint, Symacchus and the Latin versions understood it. Aquila and the Peshitta were content to transcribe this obscure word. The meaning of ceiling or joists happens to be confirmed by Arabic *rht*, "to be gathered, assembled," or "furnishings," which is the current meaning in Modern Hebrew. I. Zolli translates this word in the same way in 7:6: "*como porpora regale legata attorno a stanghe*" ("like the royal purple bound around a beam"). This is also the interpretation of L. Krinetzki:[15] "*befestigt am Gebälk (eines Königspalastes)*" ("fastened to the framework of a royal palace"). G. Gerleman translates it this way:[16] "The threads (*Fäden*) of the head are like royal purple, fastened to the wooden pillars (*an den Baümen festgemacht*)." He thinks that *dallâ* brings to mind the threads to be woven, spoken of in Isaiah 38:12, "the threads of the chain (warp) are cut." The threads in fact were connected to the frame of the weaving-loom. Gerleman concludes that the royal purple would be the thread of the weaver. But D. Lys[17] is right in asking why the poet would here describe such an attachment in speaking of a woman's hair.

Eliezer Ben Yehuda had suggested emending the Hebrew by reading *mallek* or *millek*, "your tresses."[18] Without any emendation, some translators at times render it as "tresses" by reason of the context. So M. H. Pope has: "A king captive in the tresses."[19] Another possibility is suggested by G. R. Driver who paraphrases: "Your tresses are braided with ribbons."[20] The translation of Symmachus, *eilēmasin*, "coils, cords" brings to mind the story of Samson and Delilah (Judg. 16:6ff.). Delilah bound the seven tresses of Samson's hair. The verb *'āsar*, "to bind," occurs seven times in this story; but it never means "to fasten, to secure" which would have to be expressed by other verbs (*kwn, rks, ḥzq*, etc.). The usual meaning "to bind" must be preserved in Song 7:6.

We should abandon the false parallel with 1:17 and choose others that are more enlightening: for instance, Genesis 30:38 and 41, as well as Exodus 2:16 where *rhṭ* means "drain, gutter, ditch" through which water flows rapidly to fill troughs and watering holes. It is found in Aramaic and Syriac and its general sense corresponds to the Hebrew root *rwṣ*, "to run"; we often speak of "running" water. This Aramaism is translated very well by the Septuagint, *basileus dedemenos en paradromais* ("a king is bound in the corridors"), while the Peshitta has *brhṭ* (merely transcribed), and the Vulgate, *vincta canalibus* ("bound in channels"). The Song of Songs contains many other Aramaisms.

Does this mean that the red purple would be confined in the channels (ditches)? Perhaps it may be something like the channels, ridges or grooves cut into the heads of Egyptian statues into which gold or coloring material was poured to imitate a wig. If it is true, as Gerleman[21] thinks, that some descriptions in the Song, like that of the young man (5:11ff.), took their inspiration from Egyptian statues, it must be admitted that we would have here a very subtle way to call to mind the wig of the young woman.

An Akkadian text, entitled "lyrical description" by J. Nougayrol, applies to a woman the metaphor of a channel (*rātu*, an exact equivalent of the Aramaic and Hebrew): "My mother . . . is a channel who brings an abundance of water to the flower beds." The corresponding Hittite text is translated in this way by E. Laroche: "She is like the channel; the waters run there like a torrent toward the fields."[22]

We are led therefore to see in the plural *rehāṭîm* (7:6) a metonymy to indicate water flowing in a channel. The flowing hair of the young woman is compared to the flowing of water. From this we get the translation proposed here: "A king is bound (or: a prisoner) in these tresses."[23] This comes close to the translation of D. Lys: "A king is bound by these waves,"[24] a translation found also in *TOB*.[25]

This imagery is not new. Already 4:1 and 6:5 compared the hair of the young woman to a flock of goats which stream (*glšw*) down Mount Gilead. The equivalent Ugaritic word *glt* also brings to mind the stirring up of waters, in parallelism with *thmt*, "oceans."[26] The flowing hair *streams* like the goats who run in every direction down the slopes of the hill. G. Dalman notes that the Aramaic word *glš* is used of a head of hair which billows and flows freely.[27] Nowadays, Theophile Gautier speaks of "flowing hair," while Romain Rolland writes about her ample white wig whose curls flowed wildly over her shoulders.[28]

Incidentally, the image of imprisonment in speaking of hair is a common theme in Egyptian love songs; they compare hair to a hunting net or a trap ready to spring.[29] We may also cite Apuleius: "Adjuro te per dulcem istum capilli tui nodulum, quo meum vinxisti spiritum" ("I put you under oath by the knot of your lovely hair with which you have bound fast my spirit").[30]

But who is the king bound or captive in the tresses of his well-beloved's hair? Some exegetes speak here of a parody. It would be the bridegroom who would be referred to as "King" at the moment of his marriage.[31] We should note, however, that the young woman is never called queen in the Song. She receives many compliments from queens (6:9); but they only refer to her as "daughter of a nobleman or prince's daughter" (7:2). Previously (1:4 and 12; 3:9 and 11) there was question of King Solomon. This cannot be the case in 7:6 since it is he who is supposed to be proclaiming the praise of his fiancée. Therefore, A. Robert, followed by a few other exegetes, would be inclined to see an implicit allusion here to King Hiram of Tyre. The latter had formally *bound* himself by an enduring covenant treaty to the two kings, David and Solomon.[32] It should be noted that the verb *'āsar*, "bind," and its derivative *'issār*, can be used of a contractual obligation.[33] Besides, the accumulation of geographical names at the end of the *wasf* cannot be an accident. These names recall the regions which border on Palestine, namely, the Salomonic Empire at its greatest extent (cf. p. 49). Incidentally, we know that Tyre and Cyprus carried on trade in purple fabrics (Ezek. 27:7,16).

We could even wonder whether or not the participle *'āsûr*, "bound," was chosen because it sounds like Ṣōr, Tyre. It is also interesting to note that the four consonants in the name Hiram (in Hebrew) are found in the word *reḥāṭîm*.[34] There are countless puns on proper names in the Bible.[35] We have already noted those connected with the names of Solomon, David and Moriah (4:6). The name of Lebanon leads to several puns in 4:6–9: *lebônâ*, "incense"; *libbabtinî*, "you have ravished my heart" (you drive me out of my mind). It has also been noted that the poet was able to bring to mind the divine names *'elohê ṣebā'ôt*, "God of hosts," and *šadday*, "Mighty One" (a divine name frequently used, especially in the book of Job) in the refrain of 2:7, etc.: *ṣebā'ôt*, *'ayelôt*, *śādeh*, "the gazelles, the does of the fields (wild does)." There are also the allusions to the story of Abraham or to the episode of the transfer of the ark. It was in this way that the Scribes of the Second Temple period loved, as good pedagogues, to call to mind the history of Israel through obscure words, in language that was deliberately enigmatic[36] and filled with double meanings. They sought in this way to arouse the curiosity of their hearers and to strengthen the hope in the hearts of those who awaited the full realization of the Covenant promises, at the time of the coming of the New Solomon, son of David and son of Abraham.

*

*   *

---

1   A paper on the subject of this chapter was given at the Tenth International Congress for the Study of the Old Testament in Vienna, August 27, 1980.

2   There are three other occurrences of *kaph* in verses 9–10. There were already six in the first *wasf* (4:1–5).

3   *talpîôt*, from the root *lph*, "to arrange in courses"; it is found in Aramaic and in Arabic (ROBERT-TOURNAY, p. 441; POPE, p. 467).

4   Cf. M. AVI-YONAH, "Mount Carmel and the God of Baalbeck," *IEJ* 2 (1952), p. 121.

5   B. COUROYER, "Ceux-qui-sont-sur-le-sable: les *Hériou-Shâ*," *RB* 78 (1971), p. 560.

6   Cf. *RB* 85 (1978), p. 411.

7   J. BRIEND and J.-B. HUMBERT, *Tell Keisan (1971–1976). Une cité phénicienne en Galilée* (OBO, Series Archaeologica 1), Gabalda, Vandenhoeck, Ed. universitaires de Fribourg, 1981, pp. 226–27 (E. Puech).

8   Cf. 2 Chron. 2:6–13; 3:14.

9   From the root *dll*, "to hang down" (cf. Job 28:4). The Ethiopic *delul* refers to curls which dangle; the same is true of Maltese *dliel* (J. AQUILINA, "Maltese as Mixed Language," *JSS* 3 (1958), p. 65).

10 Cf. L. B. JENSEN, "Royal Purple of Tyre," *JNES* 22 (1963), pp. 104–18; R. GRADWOHL, "Die Farben im Alten Testament," *BZAW* 83 (1963), p. 72. A. van SELMS, *UF* 2 (1970), p. 261; D. PARDEE, *ibid.* 6 (1974), pp. 277–78; J. SANMARTIN, *ibid.* 10 (1978), pp. 455–56. On the royal purple, cf. 1 Macc. 8:14.

11 Cf. Haupt, Horst, Winandy, etc.
12 O. LORETZ, *Studien zur althebräischen Poesie I. Das althebräische Liebeslied* . . . (AOAT 14/1, 1971), p. 42.
13 Cf. R. AARON HYMAN and ARTHUR B. HYMAN, *Torah hakethubah vehamessurah*, 2nd ed., Part III, *Hagiographa*, 1979, Tel Aviv, p. 183.
14 Cf. *Bib* 21 (1940), pp. 276–82.
15 Cf. *Bib* 52 (1971), p. 188.
16 *Ruth. Das Hohelied*, pp. 199–200.
17 LYS, p. 264.
18 "Three Notes in Hebrew Lexicography," *JAOS* 37 (1917), p. 324; ROBERT-TOURNAY, p. 267.
19 *Song of Songs*, 1977, pp. 593, 630.
20 *The New English Bible*, 1970, p. 805.
21 *Op. cit.*, p. 71. See above, p. 63.
22 In *Ugaritica V* (Mission de Ras Shamra, XVI, 1968), pp. 316, 774. An erotic interpretation should not be discounted.
23 NIV is close to this: "The king is held captive by its tresses." RSV, NAB and JB are very similar.
24 *Op. cit.*, pp. 225, 265. LYS refers to the *wasf* published by J. G. Wetzstein: "Her hair . . . goes out in billows." The same interpretation is found in L. KRINETZKI, *Das Hohe Lied*, 1964, p. 310.
25 *Ancien Testament*, Paris, 1975, p. 1069, note d.
26 Cf. CAQUOT-SZNYCER-HERDNER, *Textes Ougaritiques*, I, p. 207.
27 *Aramäisch-neuhebräisches Handwörterbuch*, 1922, p. 81a.
28 These quotations are from *Le Petit Robert*, Dict. alphabétique et analogique de la langue française, 1968, p. 1586.
29 We will cite two texts: "As bait for my eyes is her hair, there in the trap ready to spring." "From her hair she flings at me her nets." (Cf. S. SCHOTT, *Les chants d'amour de l'Égypte ancienne*, pp. 69, 82; ROBERT-TOURNAY, pp. 344, 349.)
30 Quoted in ROBERT-TOURNAY, p. 268.

³¹ As opposed to the opinions of G. Gerleman and D. Lys.

³² Cf. 2 Sam. 5:11; 1 Kgs. 5:15–26; 9:10–14,26–28; 10:11,22; 2 Chron. 2:2–15; JOSEPHUS, *Jewish Antiquities* 8:5,3; *Contra Apion* 1:17,18. Hiram provided Israel with purple and crimson. Workers from Tyre and Sidon worked also on the reconstruction of the Second Temple under Zerubbabel (Ezra 3:7).

³³ Cf. Num. 30:3–6, 8,11–15.

³⁴ More precisely in the interesting variant *reḥāṭîm* found in some manuscripts and the Kethib (cf. KB 876).

³⁵ Thus Micah 1:10–16 multiplied the puns on place names. L. Krinetzki has studied alliteration and paronomasia in the Song (*Das Hohe Lied*, Düsseldorf, 1964, *passim*). We may cite as an example Song 4:2, *šekullām* and *šakulāh* ("twin" and "alone"). Cf. F. M. TH. BÖHL, "Wortspiele im Alten Testament," *JPOS* 6 (1926), pp. 196–212; A. STRUS, *Nomen-Omen. La stylistique sonore des noms propres dans le Pentateuque* (AnBib 80, 1978), Rome, p. 37; Y. ZAKOWITCH, "The Synonymous Word and Synonymous Name in Name-Midrashim," *Shnaton. Annual for Biblical and Ancient Near Eastern Studies* 2 (1977), pp. 100–15 (in Hebrew); J. T. MILIK, "Daniel et Suzanne à Qumran?" *De la Tôrah au Messie, Mélanges H. Cazelles*, Paris, 1981, pp. 350–53 (play on Aramaic homonyms in the story of Susanna).

³⁶ King Hiram makes a pun on Cabul in 1 Kgs. 9:13 (cf. *RB* 64 (1967), pp. 266–67). According to Josephus (*Contra Apion*, 1:111ff. and *Jewish Antiquities* 8:50ff.), Hiram and Solomon wrote each other letters in which each proposed riddles to be solved; it is true that these letters which had been preserved at Tyre "up to this day" had doubtless been forged by Eupolemus. But they were in-

spired by the story of the Queen of Sheba (1 Kgs. 10:1ff) who came to test Solomon with riddles; he, we are told, gave her an answer to all of them. On riddles in the Bible, cf. Judg. 14:12ff.; Ezek. 17:2; Pss. 49:5 and 78:2; Prov. 1:6; Sir. 8:8 and 47:17; Dan. 5:12 and 8:23.

Chapter Ten

IMPLICIT HISTORICAL ALLUSIONS

*T*his topic, which has not yet been systematically studied, deserves an extensive treatment. However, it will have to be enough for now to mention some examples of how the sacred writers loved to recall the events in the history of Israel and her neighbors through obscure words and more or less clear allusions. Already the symbolic acts of inspired individuals, whose deeds were as efficacious as their words, had used the indirect and vivid language of expressive behavior.[1] Parallel to this, there developed in Israel a fondness for fables, riddles, parables and, to sum it all up, *māšāl*, the prerogative of the "sages."[2] Allegorical narratives such as the parables of Jotham (Judg. 9:8–15) and of Nathan (2 Sam. 12:1–4) and the fable of Jehoash (2 Kgs. 14:9–10) transformed historical facts, and later on Ezekiel did the same as he became the master in this domain of historical allegory.[3] This is how this prophet presents in several poems the last years of the Judean monarchy and the fall of Jerusalem, so that modern interpreters have often run into difficulties in interpreting some of the obscure details. Chapter 17:1–10, the allegory of the two eagles, the cedar and the vine, is concerned with Nebuchadnezzar, Psammetichus, Jehoiakim and Zedekiah; then, in the explanation that follows (verses 12ff.), there is question only of Babylon and Jerusalem, the king of Babylon and the pharaoh, but their names are not even mentioned. In the same way, the lament (*qînâ*) of chapter 19 over the princes of Israel is content with implicit allusions to Jehoahaz, Jehoiachin and Zedekiah. We could also spend a lot of time on Chapters 16 and 23 which relate in symbolic form the history of the two sisters, Jerusalem and Samaria. It is chapter 20 that narrates clearly these same events.

Such symbolic frescoes painted onto history inaugurated a whole new Hebrew and Aramaic literature which will reach its peak in the apocalypses. Chapters 7 and 8 of the book of Daniel offer two remarkable examples of this. In the midrashic literature and the Haggada, not only recent history, but the whole past history of Israel will be called to mind: the patriarchal age, the time of the Exodus, the period of the monarchy, the Exile and the return from Babylon, the Second Temple period. Endlessly occupied in reading and rereading the Sacred Scriptures, the scribes and the priests learned how to interpret the subtleties of the text, just as the rabbis will do later on. We may recall, for example, the discussions presently going on over the historical allusions contained in the *Pesher* of Habakkuk discovered at Qumran: who is the Teacher of Righteousness, the Man of Lies, the Wicked Priest?[4] It is only natural that the scribes and priests would have devoted themselves at a fairly early period to the development of this allegorical genre, so appropriate to excite curiosity and develop the talent and learning of the official interpreters of the Scriptures. The excesses of allegorical exegesis, especially in regard to the Song of Songs, should not cause us to forget or neglect certain midrashic features that can be detected in the text itself.

An important comparison may be made with the book of Qoheleth (Ecclesiastes), generally dated to the third century B.C.E., a little later than the time of composition of the Song. Qoheleth the sage makes use of a literary fiction to present himself as "the son of David, king in Jerusalem," and then begins with a self-criticism in the first two chapters of his book. As a matter of fact, the reign of the great king Solomon, so wise, rich, famous, would have been a golden age, but it ends up miserably with the catastrophe of the schism of the ten tribes from which Israel never recovered. "I detest all the work I have done under the sun and now give up to the man who succeeds me. Who knows whether he will be wise or a fool? He will be master of all my work which I will have done with my wisdom under the sun. That too is vanity" (Eccles. 2:18–19). Possibly this text has been touched up.[5] But that reediting would imply that the sages tended to historicize some passages; and this would justify all the more a search for historical allusions. The book of Kings tells how Rehoboam, son of Solomon, rejected the advice of the elders and provoked the people by threatening to increase the burden which had already weighed upon them in the time of his father Solomon. "My father punished you with whips, I will punish you with spiked lashes" (1 Kgs. 12:14).[6] Everyone knows what followed.

At the time Qoheleth wrote, the situation of the Jews in Palestine had changed considerably since the time of Ezra and Nehemiah. Prosperity and relative calm had been succeeded by a period of insecurity with the struggle between the Ptolemies and Seleucids. This put an end to the optimism and flowery lyricism of the Song. Qoheleth definitely seems to take an opposite tack right away in his book.[7] Later on, at the beginning of the second century B.C.E., Sirach (47:19ff.) does not fail to recall what an ambiguous personality Solomon was. Wise when he was young, he later on defiled his line by "abandoning his body to women." So he brought retribution on his children and made them deplore his folly. His kingdom was split in two and a rebel kingdom arose from Ephraim. Solomon left behind him "the foolishest of the people," a pun between *rābâ*, "broad," followed by *'ām*, "people," and the name of Rehoboam, *rĕhabĕ'ām* (47:23).

The second part of Zechariah, generally dated to the beginning of the Hellenistic period, does not lack allusions to either ancient or recent Israelite history. It has long been recognized that the beginning of chapter 9 recalls the expedition of Alexander the Great in Syro-Palestine.[8] The following verses evoke the coming of the King-Messiah, the new Solomon, who should bring peace to the daughter of Zion. Solomon is here idealized as in the Song of Songs and the book of Chronicles. We have not yet reached the time of Qoheleth. The same complacent and optimistic picture, developed at length, appears in Psalm 72, so much like "Second" Zechariah. Dedicated, as it should be, to Solomon, this messianic psalm draws its inspiration in its definitive form from the ancient oracles and the usual court style of the ancient East.

All the texts from the end of the fourth century clearly reflect the portrait of the expected messianic king that the Jews of that epoch were used to. Its principal characteristic was perfect serenity, peaceful behavior.

In chapter 11 of Zechariah, I have proposed that an allusion to the end of Solomon's reign be found in the allegory of the "three shepherds."[9] Verse 8, one of the most puzzling in the whole Bible, has given rise to a multitude of hypotheses: "I will get rid of the three shepherds *in just one month.* . . . " Could not these three "shepherds" simply be Solomon, Rehoboam and Jeroboam? In fact, it is in a space of just one month that the elderly Solomon died, that his son Rehoboam, the fool, summoned the assembly at Shechem, and that the usurper Jeroboam set up his golden calves at Dan and Bethel. The covenant is thoroughly torn apart (Zech. 11:10–11). The schism between the two kingdoms of the north and south, between Ephraim and Judah, is from now on complete.

It also seems possible to detect some allusions, in chapters 12–14, to the great figure of David, a type of the expected Messiah, to the activity of the prophet Elijah, to the death of Josiah, killed at Megiddo in 609, to the putting out of the eyes of Zedekiah, the last king of Judah (Zech. 11:17), to the Exile and to the return to Zion.[10]

The process of historicizing the psalter may have taken place in this same period. This tendency especially manifests itself in the "Davidic" titles which introduce thirteen psalms.[11] Nine are connected with the persecution by Saul: 7, 34, 52, 54, 56, 57, 59, 63 and 142. Psalm 3 would be about David fleeing from his son Absalom. Psalm 18 would celebrate the king's victories; Psalm 51 would relate to the murder of Uriah, and Psalm 60 to the campaign against Edom. The Septuagint has several more such titles and adds the apocryphal Psalm 151 which is found in a double and more developed form in the large scroll of psalms discovered in cave 11 at Qumran;[12] this composition especially takes its inspiration from 1 Samuel 16:1–18. In this same scroll, the "Testament of David" (2 Sam. 23) is followed by ten lines which complacently describe the literary activity of David. The latter would have composed 3,600 psalms and 450 canticles, many more than his son Solomon who, according to 1 Kings 5:12, composed 1,005 canticles (5,000 according to the Septuagint) and 3,000 proverbs.

The Levitical scribes of the Second Temple consequently speeded up the process of historicizing the psalter, and the Jewish translators at Alexandria imitated them; so the Septuagint title for Psalm 75 (Hebrew 76) then is "Concerning the Assyrian," an allusion to the siege by Sennacherib in 701. In actual fact, modern exegesis discovers in this psalm recollections of Isaiah 37:20–35; the deliverance of Jerusalem became the type and symbol of the salvation awaited by the Poor of YHWH in messianic times. Many other allusions to the history of Israel could be pointed out. We may mention for example the episode of Datan and Abiram of Numbers 16 (Psalms 55:16, 24; 140:11b and 141:7; cf. 106:17), the destruction of Sodom (Psalms 11:6 and 140:11a), the taking up of Elijah to heaven (Psalms 49:16b and 73:24b). In all these examples there is question of more or less clear indirect allusions.

Very typical of this point of view is the difficult Psalm 68, that processional hymn in which some think a catalogue of *incipits* are listed one after the other, just as in Assyro-Babylonian catalogues. However, a thorough study of the sources of this psalm lets us see instead a great lyrical fresco of the history of Israel in the form of a historical retrospective. One finds in it the principal stages in the history of the people of God.[13]

First there is the signal for the liturgical procession: Moses addressing the ark in the desert (Num. 10:35–36; cf. Is. 33:3). Of course, it could refer to a commemorative procession subsequent to the disappearance of the ark in the turmoil of 587 and the destruction of the Temple. It is possible that in verse 18,[14] "the twice thousand of thousands" (*ribbōtayim 'alfê*) corresponds to the "thousand of thousands" (*ribebôt 'alfê*) spoken of in the address of Moses (Numbers 10:36) in an unfortunately badly-preserved Hebrew text which has certainly been retouched.

In any case the psalm calls to mind the Exodus from Egypt and the journey through the desert with the theophany at Sinai (verses 5–11) together with an allusion to the manna and the quails (verse 10). The victory of Deborah and Barak, in the time of the Judges, is evoked in verses 12–14; verse 14 borrows from the Canticle of Deborah, Judges 5:16 (an example of "anthological" style). An allusion to the destruction of Shechem by Abimelech (Judges 9:46–49) may be found in verse 15, along with the Dark Mountain (Zalmon) which overlooks Shechem, and the snow which brings to mind the salt sowed on the ruins of Shechem (cf. Sirach 43:18–19).[15] Just as in the Song (2:14; etc.), the "dove" is a symbol of Israel (see page 92). The choice of Zion as a divine dwelling is mentioned in verses 16–17, while the ascent of the ark to Zion and the victories of David are recalled in verses 18–21. The mention of tens of thousands of chariots, in verse 18, makes one think of the chariotry of Solomon; 1 Kings 10:26 speaks of 1,400 chariots and of 12,000 horsemen, while 1 Kings 5:6 mentions 40,000 stalls (or teams); but 2 Chronicles 9:25 speaks of only 4,000 (see page 57). All in all, the reign of Solomon is not particularly praised by the psalmist!

Verses 23–24 next seem to recall the predictions of the prophet Elijah on the deaths of Kings Ahab and Jehoram as well as that of Queen Jezebel. The processions and choruses of verses 25–28, with the tribes of Benjamin, Judah, Zebulon and Naphtali, can call to mind the famous Passover of Hezekiah (2 Chronicles 30:1ff., where Zebulon is mentioned in verses 10, 11 and 18). The final verses of Psalm 68 fit in with the universalist concepts of the postexilic parts of the book of Isaiah, announcing the coming up of pagan kings to adore the true God in Jerusalem. But at the same time Egypt, the "Beast of the Reeds," is threatened. She who had of old oppressed the Hebrews continues to do so. Verses 31–32 must have been retouched under the stress of calamitous events such as the massive deportation of Jews to Egypt by Ptolemy I Soter around 320. This would give the *terminus ad quem* for the definitive redaction of Psalm 68. It is true that the "Beast of the Reeds" could also be the buffalo of Lake Huleh, equivalent to Behemoth of the book of Job; it would be question then of Syria of the Seleucids, the enemy from the North.[16] We are here once again led back to the time of "Second" Zechariah and Chronicles, a few decades after the presumed time of composition of the Song of Songs.

It is well known that Hebrew proper names of either persons or places easily lend themselves to word plays. As a result of this, in Genesis, for example, about sixty proper names of persons provide an opportunity for significant word plays or more or less successful paronomasia. To see this, one need only skim through the recent work of A. Strus, *Nomen-Omen.*[17] It is also well known how ingenious the scribes were in blotting out and ridiculing the names of pagan deities. The same was done to certain names particularly odious for Israel. Take, for instance, the name of Nebuchadnezzar, in Hebrew *Nebukadnessar.* The word *nēṣer,* "branch," in the cantilena about the death of an Assyro-Babylonian king (Is. 14:19) could recall the latter part of the name of the one who destroyed Jerusalem and the Temple in 587; the versions read *neṣel*, "abortion" here. This word is modified by the word "loathsome." Modern versions have taken note of this allusion.[18] The frequent occurrence of the word *ṣar*, "enemy, adversary," in the scroll of the five Lamentations could be explained in the same way. This word comes up three times in the first great national lament in the psalter: Psalm 44:6, 8,11. The majority of commentators connect this psalm with the catastrophe of 587.

When the Song of Moses speaks of a nation as "crazy," *nābāl* (Deut. 32:21), we must think of the Hebrew name for Babylon, *Bābel*;[19] the same may be the case in Psalm 74:18: "A *foolish* people insults your name."[20] The device of *Atbash*[21] permitted the transposition of *Bābel* into *Šēšak* (Jer. 25:26; 51:41). In the same way *kaśdîm* (Chaldeans) became *lēb qāmāy*, "the heart of my adversaries" (Jer. 51:1). Such cryptography is not rare in rabbinical writings which speak of Amalek or Edom to designate the enemies of the Jewish people and of their faith. The psalter had earlier offered some examples of intentional graphic retouches. We have already pointed out Psalm 68:31–32. We may add Psalm 80:14 where the "forest" has become "the river," that is, the Nile in Egypt, through the omission of the letter *'ayin* written "suspended," above the line, in the Massoretic manuscripts.[22] The Mishna thought that this was done to indicate that here was the middle of the psalter; however, the real middle is found between verses 35 and 36 of Psalm 78.

The last word in Psalm 123:4, *lg'ywnîm*, has been cut in two by the *qěrê*, indicating that it should be read *lg'y ywnym*, "for the proud among the oppressors," with *ywnym* being able to be read also as *yěwānîm*, "the Greeks"; doubtless this would involve a retouching in the time of the Maccabees to call to mind Antiochus Epiphanes.[23]

It is possible too that an explicit historical allusion might become hidden as a result of a textual retouching, intentional or not.

Here is an example that is actually not well known. In the "prayer" of Habakkuk 3:11, the phrase "the sun and moon stood still in their dwelling" doubtless recalls Joshua 10:12–13. Verse 10 had already spoken of torrential rain and thunder. So it refers to a violent storm. That is why it is possible to see here an allusion to the battle of Gibeon, when Israel crushed the Amorites. All that is needed is to consider *'mr* before the word *selâ* (Pause), in verse 9b of Habakkuk 3, as a defective writing of *'mry*, "Amorite."[24] We may then translate: "You overwhelm the arrows of the Amorite," an allusion to the huge hailstones spoken of in the Joshua narrative. The Hebrew text of Habakkuk has been re-touched with a view to liturgical usage for the feast of Pentecost, Shavuot, "the Weeks," the commemoration of the giving of the Torah on Mount Sinai. This explains the present tenor of the Massoretic Text: "Your bow is uncovered, the oaths, spears of the word (*'mr*)." Or else: "The words of the oaths are the spears."[25] Or again: "You conjure up the spears with the words."[26] "You give the string its fill of arrows" is a conjectural reading, following a Greek manuscript.[27] The liturgical rereading has obscured the original Hebrew text by changing the verb "you overwhelm," *śb't* to *śb'wt*, "oaths" or "weeks": Pentecost is the feast of Weeks. In the primitive text, the only allusion was to the victory at Gibeon, following after the mention of the Exodus trek from Sinai toward Canaan by way of the south-east of Palestine.

There are then implicit historical allusions all through the Bible. But it is often difficult to state them precisely and certainly.[28] We do not know the biblical text and biblical history as well as the scribes or their audience who could still profit from oral traditions lost to us. Prudence is needed therefore in this area; but it would be unreasonable to deny *a priori* the possibility of allusions such as those which we think we have detected in the Song of Songs, which is from a time when the sacred writers had a tendency to multiply such allusions.

✳

✳   ✳

---

¹ 1 Kgs. 11:29; 22:11; Is. 20:2; Jer. 13; 18; 27; 28; Ezek. 4; 12; 24; 37; etc.

² On the riddle, cf. J. L. CRENSHAW, "Questions, dictons et épreuves impossibles," *La Sagesse de l'Ancien Testament*, ed. M. Gilbert (BETL 51, 1979), pp. 96–111. On *Māšāl* in its many and varying forms, cf. A. GEORGE, "Parabole," *DBS* 8 (1960). col. 1149–1155.

³ Cf. W. ZIMMERLI, *Ezechiel* (BKAT XIII/1, 1969), pp. 46*–47*, 343, 378.

⁴ Cf. MURPHY-O'CONNOR, review of B. E. THIERING, *Redating the Teacher of Righteousness*, 1979, in *RB* 87 (1980), pp. 425–30.

⁵ Cf. A. LAUHA, *Kohelet*, 1978, pp. 42, 55.

⁶ Literally "scorpions."

⁷ Cf. R. TOURNAY, *RB* 69 (1962), p. 605. Eccles. 4:13–16 has been compared to the story of Joseph (Gen. 42:6) or to that of David (1 Sam. 18:23), or again to the dynastic successions of the Seleucid kings. We cannot be specific on this (cf. A. LAUHA, *Kohelet*, 1978, pp. 92–93; G. S. OGDEN, "Historical Allusion in Qoheleth, IV, 13–16," *VT* 30 (1980), pp. 309–15; N. LOHFINK, *Kohelet* (Die Neue Echter Bibel), 1980, p. 39). An allusion has also been seen in Eccles. 10:16 to Ptolemy V Epiphanes who took the throne in 205 at the age of five years (cf. N. LOHFINK, *op. cit.*, p. 78).

⁸ M. DELCOR, *RB* 63 (1956), pp. 175–81; F.-M. ABEL, *RB* 49 (1935), p. 54. Ps. 29 could refer to the same historical context, if it is not an archaic psalm but an archaizing one. Alexander's armies merely wanted to pass through Palestine (cf. R. TOURNAY, "El Salmo 29: estructura e interpreta-

cion," *Ciencia Tomista* 106 (1979): *Festschrift Colunga*, p. 750).

9 Cf. R. TOURNAY, "Zacarias 9–11 e a Historia de Israel," *Atualidades biblicas*, Ed. Vozes, Petropolis, 1971, pp. 331–49.

10 Cf. R. TOURNAY, "Zacharie XII–XIV et l'histoire d'Israël," *RB* 81 (1974), pp. 355–74.

11 See R. TOURNAY *et al.*, *Les Psaumes* (*BdJ*), 3rd edit., 1964, p. 17; E. SLOMOVIC, "Toward an Understanding of the Formation of Historical Titles in the Book of Psalms, *ZAW* 91 (1979), pp. 350–80; J. KÜHLEWEIN, *Geschichte in den Psalmen*, Calwer Verlag, Stuttgart, 1973.

12 J. A. SANDERS, *The Psalms Scroll of Qumran Cave 11* (*11QPsª*), "Discoveries in the Judean Desert of Jordan," IV, 1965.

13 See the notes in *Psaumes* (*BdJ*), 3rd edit., pp. 289–95.

14 The Hebrew *šine'ān*, "repetition" (according to the Aramaic) is translated "tranquil" in the Septuagint which read *ša'anān* (with one Hebrew manuscript). Syriac translated it "army" (*dḥyl'*). It has been compared to Ugaritic *tnn*, a sort of soldier, archer? (CAQUOT-SZNYCER-HERDNER, *Textes Ougaritiques* I, 1974, p. 517; cf. *RB* 75 [1968], p. 438). Comparison has also been made with Arabic *sana*, "to shine" (J. GRAY, *JSS* 22 [1977], p. 2). TOB and CAQUOT translate: "Two myriads of flaming squadrons."

15 Cf. R. TOURNAY, "Le Psaume LXVIII et le livre des Juges," *RB* 66 (1959), pp. 358–68.

16 See B. COUROYER, "Le 'glaive' de Béhémoth: Job XL, 19–20," *RB* 84 (1977), p. 59.

17 Analecta Biblica 80, Rome, 1978 (see above, p. 86 and note 34). Cf. also L. ALONSO-SCHÖKEL, art. "Poésie hébraïque," *DBS* 8, col. 60.

18 For example, *TOB*, p. 782, note i, following *BdJ*, p. 1108, note a. *JB*, p. 1213, note f. H. WILDBERGER (*Jesaja*, BKAT X/2, p. 542) considers this allusion uncertain.

[19] R. TOURNAY, *RB* 67 (1980), p. 122. The Targum of Pseudo-Jonathan and the Midrash already identify the foolish people with the Babylonians (cf. S. CARRILLO ALDAY, *El Cantico de Moises* (DT 32), Madrid, 1970, p. 92).

[20] *Les Psaumes*, 3rd edit., p. 317, note 1.

[21] *Atbash* is a cipher by which letters of one name, counted from the beginning of the Hebrew alphabet, are exchanged for corresponding letters counted from the end.

[22] H.-J. KRAUS (*Psalmen I*, 1960, p. 559) mentions the hypothesis according to which it would refer to the expedition of Pharao Nechao in the time of King Josiah.

[23] Cf. earlier E. KÖNIG, *Die Psalmen*, 1927, p. 362.

[24] Cf. R. TOURNAY, *RB* 72 (1965), p. 428; *ibid.*, 77 (1970), p. 624; 80 (1973), p. 300. P. JÖCKEN (*Das Buch Habakuk, BBB* 48, 1977, pp. 352–53, 356) mentions this hypothesis.

[25] This is the interpretation of the *TOB*, p. 1201 and note 1. The same ambiguity is found in Jer. 5:24; cf. H. WEIPPERT, *Schöpfer des Himmels und der Erde* (Stuttgarter Bibelstudien 102), 1981, pp. 91–92.

[26] C.-A. KELLER, *Nahum, Habacuc, Sophonie*, 1971, p. 172.

[27] *JB*, 1985, p. 1565, note m.

[28] One can see in Proverbs 28:12,15,16,17,21 allusions to the time of Jezebel and Athaliah as well as to the intrigues that marked the transitory reigns of the last kings of Israel (*TOB*, p. 1574, note v). Hosea brings this dark period to mind in 7:3. Some have even seen in Hosea 13:10 an allusion to King Hosea (732–34) whose name means "YHWH saves": "Your king, where is he now, to save you?" (cf. *JB*, p. 1513, note g).

Chapter Eleven

POLYSEMY AND DOUBLE ENTENDRE

*I*n the preceding chapters we have tried to show how the Hebrew text of the Song of Songs lends itself to an objectively based ambivalent reading. The prior condition is to consider the Song as it appears in the Judeo-Christian tradition, namely, as a "biblical" book. A *double level* is then perceptible, just as in so many poetical works in the ancient and modern Near East. Human love, between man and woman, is found expressed there in its most carnal reality, exactly as in the secular love songs of the Egyptians, Arabs and others, but in a language which revives the idea of divine love, the language of the Davidic and Messianic Covenant; all this suggests a second level.

This refined, sophisticated writing, with a learned and difficult stock of words producing such delicate sonorous effects, has two levels which, far from mutually excluding one another, overlap and intertwine in an almost indissoluble way. Quite correctly the Fathers of the Church and theologians have seen here a starting point for the Pauline teaching on marriage.

A quick glance at recent commentaries confirms the fact that modern exegesis has for a long time recognized the complexity of the hermeneutical problem presented by the Song. M. A. van den Oudenrijn[1] and G. Nolli[2] have accepted the double meaning of the Song of Songs. J. Angénieux[3] thinks that this love song had this double literal meaning right from its first composition by the poet. P. Grelot has spoken of its fuller literal sense;[4] according to him, the inspired editor had already intentionally connected this fuller meaning to the text of the poems of love in dependence on

148

the prophetic symbolism of marriage: "How could the transmission of these songs of love among the Jewish people take place without undergoing the lateral influence of the symbolism attached to love by prophetic theology, especially if they are from the time of Solomon? How could their editing as a sacred book take place without this symbolism having any part in determining their meaning? Is not the Song one example where the problem of the relationship between Scripture, seen at the level of its original composition, and the interpretative tradition in which its meaning has undergone a progressive growth, is not this one instance where the problem is faced most sharply? It will be claimed that the problem is more theological than exegetical. But what is this then but exegesis considered as a hermeneutic of the Word of God?"[5]

The symbolism of the land as wife and city as woman is deeply rooted in the Mesopotamian and Syro-Canaanite milieu. There is no need to quote here the well-known texts from Sumerian, Assyro-Babylonian and Ugaritic literature, so often compared to the oracles of Hosea, Jeremiah (for example, Jeremiah 3:1) and the book of Isaiah (for example, Isaiah 62:4). The theme of the city as woman has already been referred to above (page 48). The final editor or redactor of the Song of Songs could not avoid setting this text in the traditional context and offering it to the Jewish community, to the pious inhabitants of Jerusalem, to the temple personnel, in the light of the other sacred biblical writings, and that would have taken place right from the official acceptance by those responsible for the present book.

It is in this way, for example, that a certain ambivalence became possible about Song 5:1: "Drink, drink well, dear ones." Some commentators have been able to speak here of a spiritual inebriation and have thought that they could perceive an allusion to the oracle of Isaiah 55:1 (and parallels). They were led in this way to transpose the invitation of the Song in the perspective of the eschatological banquet spoken of in Isaiah 25:6; 65:13; Zechariah 9:17 and in some psalms (22:27; 23:5; 36:9). Passing by several texts in Philo, we can cite here a passage from the eleventh Ode of Solomon: "I am inebriated with the living and immortal waters, and my inebriation is not irrational." A fragment of a liturgical hymn, in the Bodmer Papyrus XII, seems to allude to Song 5:1: "Drink the wine, fiancée and fiancé."[6] As for St. Paul, he recommends to Christians "not *to get drunk with wine* where they find only dissipation, but to seek their *fullness* in the Spirit" (Eph. 5:19). As is known, the theme of spiritual inebriation happens to be referred to in a subtle and indirect way in the Arabic poems of Ibn-Farid (1182–1235) and in those of other Muslim mystics on the subject of wine and love.[7]

✳

✳   ✳

Exegetes of the Song could reach a satisfactory resolution of their frequently so impassioned debate according as the Song is considered to be not an allegory nor even a parable, but is acknowledged to have a "messianic" meaning: from Solomon with his Egyptian wife we move to Solomon awaited by the daughter of Zion. The tenth century B.C.E. in this case gives way to the fourth century. The idealized remembrance of the great monarch gave rise to the hope in the future peaceful King. As a consequence of this, all through the Song, in its ultimately intended meaning, there is movement from one level to the other.

The very personality of King Solomon lends itself to such ambiguity. This "peaceful" king is also the model of the sages of Israel for the annalists and the literati who attribute to him the didactic writings, namely, the book of Proverbs, Ecclesiastes and the book of Wisdom. There was a great impetus then to consider the Song of Songs a wisdom writing, teaching the goodness and value of love. Some exegetes stress this didactic aspect.[8] In fact, the feminine personification of Wisdom is a traditional motif in Jewish thought. Already in Proverbs 4:6–9, Wisdom is presented as a wife to be loved and embraced. In Proverbs 7:4 the teacher urges his disciple to say to Wisdom: "You are my sister," a way of speaking to indicate the well-beloved both in the Song and in Egyptian love songs. In the same way in Sirach 15:2, Wisdom comes to meet the Doctor of the Law like a mother and receives him as if she were a virgin bride (Hebrew: bride of her youth). In Wisdom 8:2, Solomon declares in regard to Wisdom: "Wisdom I loved and searched for from my youth; I resolved to have her as my bride and I fell in love with her beauty."[9]

The same theme is developed in the acrostic poem of Sirach 51:13–30.[10] There one finds phrases with double-meaning which could be applied as well to wisdom and piety as to physical embraces and eroticism, at least in the first part, because the second part (verses 23–30) is an exhortation to search after wisdom. In the Psalms Scroll from Cave 11 at Qumran, this poem is found between Psalm 138 and the Apostrophe to Zion (columns 21–22). This Hebrew text differs to some extent from that preserved in a manuscript discovered in the Cairo Genizah, whose verses have been jumbled: verse 15 is placed between verses 13b and 13c and is followed by 16b, while 16a is missing. The Septuagint translation was done shortly after 117 B.C.E. from a Hebrew text that is at least a century older than the Qumran text; but that older Hebrew text had been revised, because the Greek, in verses 18–20, has no more than eight hemistichs instead of the ten in the Hebrew text from Qumran, and the text is quite different in every way; there is no longer any ambiguity left in the Septuagint. It will be useful therefore to have an exact translation of the Hebrew text from Qumran, a text superior to the other two witnesses for this poem; however, the authenticity of the poem has been debated, for it could be question of an appendix to the book of Ben Sira:

13. When I was a young man,
    before I had gone astray I sought her.
14. She came to me in her beauty
    and to the end I will pursue her.
15. As the blossom fades when the grapes ripen,
    the heart is joyful.
    My foot walks on level ground
    for from my youth I have known her.
16. I inclined my ear but a little
    and I found an abundance of instruction.
17. She was for me a (glorious) yoke
    and I give honors to the one who taught me.[11]
18. I willingly planned to be zealous for good
    and I will not give up on this.
19. I burned with desire for her
    and I am not turning my face away from her.
    I stirred up[12] my desire for her
    and on her heights I will not slacken.
    My hand opened (her gate)
    and I came to know her secrets.
20. (For her) I purified my hands
    (and in her purity I found her).
    (With her from the beginning, I received under-
        standing,)
    that is why (I will not be forsaken).[13]

Comments

  −Verse 15 has been compared to the Mishna (Nid. 5:7) where the sages compare the sexual development of women with the three stages in the maturation of figs (*paggā, bōḥal, ṣemel*).–Instead of translating *'lh* by "yoke" in verse 17a (as in verse 26a and Sirach 6:30), some suggest translating it as "nurse"; but in the Bible, the word designates an animal who suckles, and never a woman. As this stich is short, it is tempting to follow the Cairo manuscript which adds *kbwd*, "glory," parallel with *hwd'h*, "honor," and makes *'lh* (masculine), "yoke," the subject of *hyh*, "is"; in the Qumran manuscript, the verb *hyth*, "is," has wisdom understood as its feminine subject.–Proverbs 5:13 seems to have inspired verses 16a and 17b: "I have not listened to the voice of my masters and I would not listen to those who taught me."–It should be noted that *lqh*, "instruction," may occur in a context on seduction, as in Proverbs 7:21 and 16:21.

Some lay stress on the conclusion of verse 19 which would contain a euphemism: "My hand opened her gate," because of the ambiguity of the word *m'rmyh* which can mean "secret parts, nudity" (2 Chronicles 28:15) or "secrets" (Sirach 42:18). The word *rwmyh* (verse 19d), "exaltation," from which the word "heights" is obtained, has also been understood as "orgasm"; but the poet could be dependent on Proverbs 8:2: "at the top of the heights . . . she takes her stand." Moreover, it has been noted that the words used in this poem are close to those in Proverbs 8:2–6. Instead of *brwmyh*, "on her heights," the Cairo manuscript has "forever," and the Septuagint has "toward the summit."

Verse 20 has to be completed by the Cairo manuscript and the Septuagint and has two possible meanings: "by keeping myself pure (in *the* state of purity), I found her"; or instead: "I found her in *her* purity," namely, "without sexual blemish," or "still a virgin."

Verse 21 preserved in the Cairo manuscript reads: "My innermost being burned like an oven to look for her."[14] This reminds us of Song 5:4: "My beloved has passed his hand through the slot, and for him my innermost being quivers." The Greek does not have the comparative phrase "like an oven"; this was doubtless added in the Cairo manuscript because of the mistake in reading *ḥmm* (to burn) instead of *ḥmm* (to quiver).

As can be seen, there is no need to give an erotic meaning to this or that phrase. Neither is there any indication of euphemisms in "my foot, my hand, my palms."

The Qumran text does not explicitly mention Wisdom but presents it here as a feminine personification (the Cairo manuscript only mentions it by name in verse 25). However, the passion of the disciple for Wisdom is assimilated to that of a man for a woman as in the other biblical texts. Lady Wisdom can therefore celebrate her "nuptials."

Symbolic descriptions of Wisdom personified have been seen in the descriptions of the lawful wife (Proverbs 5:15ff.) and the perfect mistress of the house (Proverbs 31). The sages of Israel loved to borrow from romantic poetry certain features which they would apply to Lady Wisdom. It is in this way, for example, that T. Sheppard[15] has compared Sirach 24:13 to several verses of the Song where the same motifs are found: garden, trees, perfumes, fountains, Lebanon, flowers, fruit. G. Gerleman[16] has compared the Song to the description of the womanly features of Lady Wisdom in the hymns of the Acts of Thomas.

We may recall that rabbinical exegesis had no problem in admitting a multiplicity of meanings in the Bible. According to Psalm 62:12, God can speak of two things with just one word: "Once God has spoken, twice have I heard." The rabbis generally distinguish three senses: *pešaṭ*, "simple, direct," *deraš*, "applied, homiletic," *sod*, "mystical."[17] Whatever the rabbinic ideas may be, it cannot be denied that symbols and metaphors are polyvalent by their very nature. All true poetry involves multiple harmonious elements. If a love poem can be transformed into a work on Wisdom, it can also be transformed into a work with a messianic overtone. It will be up to the reader to lean toward one meaning or toward another. The important thing will be to maintain the possibility of *double entendre*. While one avoids lapsing into the subtle and esoteric, it is only reasonable not to reduce the Song of Songs to a merely rustic romance or erotic poem.

It is necessary to recall that the Israelite sages were fond of seeking out ambiguous and polyvalent expressions to excite the curiosity of the reader. One could multiply examples of this.

In Song 2:12, *zāmîr* can be understood to mean "song" or instead "pruning of the vine" (cf. page 92).[18] In Proverbs 8:30, the word *'āmôn* can be translated "master craftsman, architect" or rather "beloved child," according as one thinks of the formation of the cosmos or more simply of the gambols of the little girl Wisdom before her father, the Creator. Neither of these meanings should be excluded.[19]

In Ecclesiastes 3:11, the word *'ōlām* has been understood in various ways: duration, eternity, world, something hidden and secret, ignorance. All these meanings can be based on usage or etymology. Ordinarily *'ōlām* refers to an indefinite duration and here the interpretation depends on the antecedent given to the word *blbm*, "in their heart." If the antecedent is human beings, what is said is that God gives them a certain understanding of events, a certain feeling for, and a partial view of, the history of the world. But the context suggests rather the duration of beings created by God who has made everything good in its time and has added to all that, in the depth of these beings, a certain permanence, a continuity in development; this is true of both humanity and the rest of nature.[20]

In chapter 12 of Qoheleth, old age is described in a succession of images and metaphors that are at times disconcerting. Commentators are very divided over their meaning. Rabbinic exegesis was fond of seeing a physiological allegory in which there would be question of arms, knees, teeth, eyes, heart, sexual desire. Other interpreters maintain that the text should be understood in the direct literal sense. Others finally admit that the poem embellishes its description with an incessant coming and going of metaphors. Without doubt it is necessary to guard against an *a priori* exclusion here of this or that interpretation; instead the reader must be allowed to taste as desired this unique masterpiece.[21] We may note that *bwr'yk*, usually translated "your creator," brings to mind *bwr*, "pit, grave," at the end of verse 6.

The first two discourses of Eliphaz, in chapters 4 and 5 of the book of Job, contain words and phrases susceptible of double meaning. This fact was pointed out some years ago by K. Fullerton and has just been studied anew by Y. Hoffman.[22] For example, the words *yir'ātekā* and *kislātekā* (4:6) are ambiguous and can be understood as meaning "your piety" or "your fear" (*yir'ātekā*) and "your foolishness" or "your hope" (*kislātekā*). In the same way, in 4:8 and 5:6, *'āwen* and *'āmāl* can be understood as meaning "sorrow" or "sin." There are two possible translations for 4:17: "Is the mortal more just than God," or rather "Is the mortal just before God," which would give the passage a completely different meaning. In 5:2, *kā'as* can be understood as meaning "spite" or "offense."

Neither were the authors of historical works afraid to use ambiguous terms or phrases.[23] Were they always even aware of this? We may doubt it. In 1 Chronicles 15:22 and 27, the word *maśśā'* can have several meanings. Was Chenaniah, the leader of the Levites, to direct the transfer of the ark, or to raise his voice (as the Septuagint understood it) to give the tone, or even to give a prophetic oracle? As is known, the activity of the Levitical singers is often described as an activity inspired by the Spirit of YHWH and quasi-prophetic.[24] In the prophetic books, the word *maśśā'* serves as a title for many oracles (Isaiah 13:1; etc.). Since it is derived from the verb *nāśā'*, "to raise," it can denote a raising of the voice, a proclamation; but also "a burden to bear." Jeremiah

23:33–40 thoroughly exploits this ambiguity: "burden" (literal sense), "oracle" (figurative sense).[25]

The oracle of Micah 5:2: "He *will give them up* until the time when she who is in labor gives birth" has been compared to the famous Emmanuel oracle (Isaiah 7:14): "This is why the Lord *will give* you a sign. . . . " Quite rightly it has been noted that the verb *ntn* lends itself here to a word play: give/give up.[26]

In Isaiah 55:3, the expression *ḥasdê David* can be understood as meaning "the good deeds of David," namely, "the proofs of his piety" (cf. 1 Maccabees 2:57) as in the case of Hezekiah (2 Chronicles 32:32) or Josiah (2 Chronicles 35:26); or instead, "the favors granted to David" (as in Psalm 89:50 and 2 Chronicles 6:42). The two meanings are both possible and do not exclude one another.[27] Modern exegesis recognizes the polyvalency of themes such as those of Emmanuel or the Servant of YHWH; these are open to so many interpretations that there seems to be no end to examinations and evaluations of their complexity. It is not rash to think that the inspired writers in Israel have always cultivated such ambiguities. Their counterparts in surrounding cultures systematically cultivated enigmas and double meanings in order to avoid being convicted of falsehood or error.

We may add some examples from the psalter. The verb *šûb*, "recover, return," is receptive of many meanings, according to its various verbal forms, even to being no more than a simple auxiliary verb of repetition.[28] Ambiguity is therefore frequent. Thus, in Psalm 60:3b, we may translate: "you will bring us back/you will make us come back/you will restore us, etc." with an allusion to the return from Babylonian Exile. But if one restores the *waw* consecutive as in some Hebrew manuscripts and the Septuagint, one can translate it as as perfect: "you have made us turn our back/ you have made us escape/you have dispersed us, etc," with an allusion to the flight mentioned in verse 6; this is the meaning of this verb form in Ezekiel 38:4,8 and 39:2. It may rightly be asked whether the psalmist has not intentionally chosen this verb with a double meaning. In fact, he multiplies the word plays in Psalm 60. In verse 5, *qāšâ*, "hard," resembles *qōšet*, "bow" or "archer," or in Aramaic, "truth";[29] at the end of verse 5, there is a wordplay of *qāšâ* with the following verb *hišqîtanû*, "you have given us to drink." In verse 6, *nes*, "signal" and *hitnôsēs*, "to flee/to zigzag, to swing in every direction" (cf. Zechariah 9:16)[30] form a paronomasia, like *'Edôm* (verse 11b) and *'ādām*, "man" (verse 13b), *māṣôr*, "citadel" (verse 11a) and *miṣṣār*, "oppression" (verse 13a). In verse 10c, the verb *hitrō'ā'y* can be understood in two ways: this form can be derived from *rw'*, "to cry" (from it therefore comes *tĕrû'â*, a war cry become a liturgical acclamation);[31] or instead from *r''*, an Aramaic verb corresponding to the Hebrew *rṣṣ*, "break." The TOB therefore superimposes these two meanings when it translates: "Against me, Philistia, bust a gut with your shouting." In the recension of Psalm 60:10 in Psalm 108:10, the ambiguity has been done away with, because the verb is in the first person, "I utter a cry against Philistia"; however, the Septuagint read the same verb form here as in Psalm 60:10.

The Aramaic verb *r''*, "to break," gives rise to ambiguity once again in Psalm 2:9. Instead of the received text, "you will break them with an iron scepter," the Septuagint understood "you will feed them with an iron scepter," as if it were the verb *r'h*, "to feed." Psalm of Solomon 17:24 supports the Masoretic reading. The author of Psalm 2 could have intended this ambiguity, because he adds in verse 10: "And now, kings, *understand*," as if he were telling them to understand well the oracle which preceded. The author of Revelation who quotes the Greek text of Psalm 2 (Revelation 2:27 and 12:5) seems to understand it according to the meaning of the Hebrew, for 19:15 speaks of striking the nations.[32] We may note also the wordplay in Proverbs

18:24 between the verb *r*ʿ, "to break" and *rēʿîm*, "comrades, friends": "Whoever has many friends will be divided by them."

A double meaning is also possible in Psalm 59:16, where *ylynw* can be translated "they spend the night" (Syriac, Symmachus, Targum), or instead, "they howl" (Septuagint, Aquila, Jerome), depending on whether that verb form comes from *lyn*, "spend the night" or from *lwn*, "to howl." In Psalm 49:13 and 21, there is also a wordplay between the verb *ylyn*, "he spends the night" and *ybyn*, "he understands."

In Psalm 126:1b, *keḥōlmîm*, "like those who dream," can also be understood as "like those who are cured, invigorated" with the Targum.[33] The verb *ḥlm* can have both meanings.

It would be easy to multiply these examples. Many Hebrew roots have a complex semantic background; many resemble each other and this permits multiple paronomasia.[34] If the Old Testament abounds in expressions with multiple meanings, it is not surprising that the same is true of the Song of Songs. We should not forget that all poetical language implies a certain polysemy.[35] And when it is God who speaks to people through divinely inspired biblical texts, will there not be many things in that message that words will be powerless to express, so profound and unutterable is the mystery of divine Love!

*

* *

[1] *Vom Sinne des Hohen Liedes, Biblische Beiträge* (H. XIV), Freiburg, 1953 (from *Divus Thomas* 31, 1953, pp. 257–80); *Het Hooglied* (De Bocken van het Oude Testament, Deel VIII/ Boek III), 1962.

² *Cantico dei Cantici* (La Sacra Bibbia), Turin, 1967. L. KRINETZKI (*Das Hohe Lied*, 1964) had also adopted this approach; but he later retracted it and no longer saw anything in the Song but a collection of love songs: " 'Retractationes' zu früheren Arbeit über das Hohe Lied," *Bib* 52 (1971), pp. 176–89; "Die erotische Psychologie des Hohen Liedes," *ThQ* 150 (1970), pp. 404–16. P. MÜLLER speaks of ambivalence ("Die lyrische Reproduktion des Mythischen im Hohenlied," *ZTK* 73 (1976), p. 40).

³ "Structure du Cantique des Cantiques," *ETL* 41 (1965), p. 142, note 53.

⁴ "Le sens du Cantique des Cantiques," *RB* 71 (1964), p. 55.

⁵ P. GRELOT, *RB* 73 (1966), pp. 129–30 (review of G. GERLEMAN, *Ruth. Das Hohelied*).

⁶ Cf. J. CARMIGNAC, "Les affinités qumrâniennes de la onzième Ode de Salomon," *RevQ* 3 (1961), p. 85, note 44; H. LEWY, *Methē nefalios. Untersuchungen zur Geschichte der Antiken Mystik*, Giessen, 1929; H. PREISKER, art. *"Methē"* in *TDNT*, IV, 545; M. TESTUZ, *Papyrus Bodmer* X–XII, 1959, pp. 63–77.

⁷ According to G. RICCIOTTI, *Il Cantico dei Cantici*, 1928, pp. 123–35; cf. A. FEUILLET, *RB* 68 (1961), p. 22, note 44; R. TOURNAY, *RB* 86 (1979), p. 139. See *Encyclopédie de l'Islam*, II (1965), art. "Ghazal," p. 1058; IV (1978) art. "Khamriyya," pp. 1038–39. And earlier, ROBERT-TOURNAY, pp. 413ff. P. GRELOT has recalled how Chinese scholars interpreted the peasant songs of the Book of Verse (Che King) in a moral sense by joining to them Confucian Commandments (*Le couple humain dans l'Écriture*, 1962, p. 67; M. GRANET, *Fêtes et chansons anciennes de la Chine*, Paris, 1919).

⁸ For example, A.-M. Dubarle, J. Winandy, J.-P. Audet, etc. See R. MURPHY, "A Biblical Model of Human Intimacy:

the Song of Songs," *Concilium* 121 (1979), pp. 61–66; O. LORETZ, "Zum Problem des Eros in Hohenlied," *BZ* 8 (1964), pp. 191–216.

9 Cf. P. BEAUCHAMP, "Épouser la sagesse ou n'épouser qu'elle? Une énigme du livre de la Sagesse," *La Sagesse de l'Ancien Testament*, ed. M. Gilbert (*BETL* 51, 1979), pp. 347–69; P. BONNARD, "De la Sagesse personifiée dans l'A.T. à la Sagesse en personne dans le Nouveau," *ibid.*, pp. 117–49.

10 This poem brings to mind Sirach 6:18–37 and 24:1–34. See the Qumran text in J. A. SANDERS, *The Psalm Scroll of Qumran Cave 11 (11 QPsª)*, 1965; also in T. MURAOKA, "Sir. 51:13–30: An Erotic Hymn to Wisdom?" *Journal for the Study of Judaism in the Persian, Hellenistic and Roman Period* 10 (1979), pp. 166–78 (with the Hebrew text of the Cairo manuscript and the Septuagint Version). *TOB* gives the translation of the Greek text of the Septuagint, pp. 2213–15. See M. DELCOR, "Le texte hébreu du cantique du Siracide LI, 13 et ss et les anciennes versions," *Textus* 6 (1968), pp. 27–47; J. A. SANDERS, "The Sirach 51 Acrostic," *Hommages à A. Dupont-Sommer*, 1971, pp. 429–38; POPE, pp. 110–11. Several authors have concluded that there is the possibility of an erotic meaning: A. DI LELLA, review of J. A. Sanders, *The Psalm Scroll of Qumran Cave 11*, *CBQ* 28 (1966), pp. 92–95 and *The Hebrew Text of Sirach*, London, 1966, pp. 101–05 (with bibliography on the question of the authenticity of the poem, p. 101, n. 80); I. RABINOWITZ, "The Qumran Hebrew Original of Ben Sira's Concluding Acrostic on Wisdom," *HUCA* 42 (1971), pp. 173–84; P. W. SKEHAN, "The Acrostic Poem in Sirach 51:13–30," *HTR* 64 (1971), pp. 387–400. See also TH. MIDDENDORP, *Die Stellung Jesu Ben Sira zwischen Judentum und Hellenismus*, Leiden, 1973, pp. 118–24.

11 Instead of *hwdw*, "his honor," Sanders reads *hwdy*, "my virility" and compares Prov. 5:9. But there is question here of giving his honor to others, and not to a stranger.

12 *ṭrty* would be for *ṭrdty* (Sanders, Baumgartner, Muraoka); a derivation from *ṭrḥ*, "to be fresh" does not give a satisfactory meaning ("to refresh"?).

13 The Qumran text is here completed by the Cairo manuscript and the Greek. These additions are in brackets.

14 Cf. Is. 16:11; Jer. 31:20; 48:36. D. WINTON THOMAS (*JTS NS* 20 [1969], pp. 225f.) suggests reading *kinnôr* in place of *tannûr* following Is. 16:11; cf. T. MURAOKA, *op. cit.*, p. 173.

15 "Wisdom as a Hermeneutical Construct," *BZAW* 151 (1980), pp. 33 and 53–54. In an incantation on love written in Akkadian there are also themes on going down into the garden, on perfumes for the lips or shoulders (cf. J. and A. WESTENHOLZ, "Help for Rejected Suitors, The Old Akkadian Love Incantation MAD V 8," *Orientalia* 46 (1977), p. 217).

16 "Bemerkungen zum Brautlied der Thomasakten," *ASTI* 9 (1973), pp. 14–22. We should note that, in a fragmentary text from Cave 4 at Qumran, a sect that was a rival of the Essenes is presented with the characteristics of a prostitute (cf. J. CARMIGNAC, "Poèmes allégoriques sur la secte rivale," *RevQ* 5/3 (1965), pp. 361–74; A. M. GAZOV-GINZBERG, "Double-Meaning in a Qumran Work ('The Wiles of the Wicked Woman')," *ibid.*, 6/2 (1967), pp. 278–85.

17 Cf. *Sanh.* 34a. See J. BONSIRVEN, *Exégèse rabbinique et exégèse paulinienne*, 1939, pp. 36 and 155; ISAAK HEINEMANN, *Altjüdische Allegoristik*, Berichte des jüdisch-theologischen Seminar für das Jahr 1935, Breslau; E. LOEWE, "Midrashim and Patristic Exegesis of the Bible," *Studia*

Patristica I, 1957, pp. 508ff. Already at Qumran, the *Midrash Pesher* practiced this kind of exegesis (cf. E. SLOMOVIC, "Towards an Understanding of the Exegesis in the Dead Sea Scrolls," *RevQ* 7/1 [1969], pp. 3–15). According to a rabbinic tradition each biblical verse would have seventy meanings.

18 H. W. WOLFF (*Hosea*, Hermeneia, Philadelphia, 1974, p. 199) rejects the play on words proposed by G. R. Driver (cf. *Canaanite Myths and Legends*, Edinburgh, 1956, p. 133) for *'aḥăbâ*, "love"/"leather" (Arabic *'ihab*) in Hosea 11:4 and later in Song 3:10; see POPE, p. 445. D. GROSSBERG sees a word with a double meaning here ("Canticles 3:10 in the Light of a Homeric Analogue and Biblical Poetics," *BTB* 11 (1981), pp. 74–76).

19 Cf. P. BONNARD, *art. cit.*, p. 38, note 145; ALAN MITCHELL COOPER, *Biblical Poetics: A Linguistic Approach*, Yale, 1976, p. 135. In Song 7:2 and Jer. 52:15, *'ammān* means craftsman. Some have seen a demythologizing of the Egyptian goddess Maat or even the god Amon in this passage (cf. Jer. 46:25; Nah. 3:8).

20 Cf. C. F. WHITLEY, *Koheleth, His Language and Thought* (BZAW, 148), 1979, pp. 31–32; A. LAUHA, *Kohelet* (BKAT XIX), 1979, pp. 68–69; E. PODECHARD, *L'Ecclésiaste* (Études Bibliques), 1912, pp. 292–95.

21 Cf. A. LAUHA, *op. cit.*, pp. 207 and 211–13; C. F. WHITLEY, *op. cit.*, pp. 96–101.

22 K. FULLERTON, "Double Entendre in the First Speech of Eliphaz," *JBL* 49 (1930), pp. 230–74; Y. HOFFMAN, "The Use of Equivocal Words in the First Speech of Eliphaz (Job IV–V)," *VT* 30 (1980), pp. 114–19.

23 Cf. Y. ROTH, "The Intentional Double-Meaning Talk in Biblical Prose," *Tarbiz* 41 (1972), p. 1 (English Summary).

24 Cf. ROBERT P. CARROLL, *When Prophecy Failed*, 1970, p. 172; D.

L. PETERSEN, *Late Israelite Prophecy* (SBL 23), 1977, p. 63; F. MICHAELI, *Les livres des Chroniques, d'Esdras et de Néhémie* (Commentaire de l'A.T., XVI), 1967, p. 90, n. 6.

25 Cf. W. MCKANE, "*MŚ*" in Jeremiah 23, 33–40" in *Prophecy. Essays Presented to G. Fohrer*, 1980, pp. 35–54.

26 Cf. B. RENAUD, *La formation du livre de Michée* (Études Bibliques), 1977, p. 247.

27 Cf. *TOB*, p. 862, note 1: 2 Chron. 6:42. P. BORDREUIL, following A. CAQUOT and many others, examines this text in *VT* 31 (1981), pp. 73–75 and compares it to Neh. 13:14. Is. 56–66 contains many plays on words (*TOB*, p. 870, note b, refers to 57:6; 58:10; 59:18; 63:3,4,6; 65:5,11; 66:20). Cf. D. F. PAYNE, "Characteristic Word Play in 'Second Isaiah.' A Reappraisal," *JSS* 12 (1967), pp. 207–29.

28 Cf. W. L. HOLLADAY, *The Root šûbh in the Old Testament with Particular Reference to its Usages in Covenantal Contexts*, Leiden, 1958; J. GRAY, *The Biblical Doctrine of the Reign*, Edinburgh, 1979, pp. 110–16. Note for example Ps. 80:4,8,15,20 and Ps. 85:2,4,5,7,9.

29 Aquila and the Targum chose this last meaning (cf. Prov. 22:21).

30 This is also the meaning of Akkadian *nasasu*.

31 Cf. P. HUMBERT, *La Terou'a*, Neuchâtel, 1946; H. P. MÜLLER, "Die kultische Darstellung der Theophanie," *VT* 14 (1964), pp. 184–88.

32 Cf. M.-E. BOISMARD, *L'Apocalypse* (BdJ), 1972, 4th edit., p. 34, note 3; G. WILHELM, "Der Hirt mit der eisernen Szepter, Überlegungen zu Psalm II 9," *VT* 27 (1977), pp. 196–204.

33 Cf. J. STRUGNELL, *JTS* 7 (1956), pp. 239–43, quoted by M. MANNATI in *Semitica* 29 (1979), p. 95.

34 Examples of paronomasia: 2 Sam. 1:20; 3:33–34; Mic. 1:10ff.; Is. 5:7; Lam. 1:16; Pss. 5:10; 25:16; 40:18; 56:9; 60:5–6;

69:30; 70:6; 74:19; 80:10; 86:1; 88:10,16. On paronomasia in the Old Testament, see Immanuel M.
CASANOWICZ, *Paronomasia in the Old Testament*, 1892; G.
R. DRIVER, "Problems and Solutions," *VT* 4 (1954), pp.
240–45; M. DAHOOD, *Psalms II, 51–100*, 1968, pp. 78,
258; W. L. HOLLADAY, "Form and Word-Play in David's
Lament over Saul and Jonathan," *VT* 20 (1970), pp. 153–
89; M. FISHBANE, "Jeremiah IV, 23–26 and Job III, 3–
13," *VT* 21 (1971), pp. 161–62; S. GEVIRTZ, "Of Patriarchs and Puns: Joseph at the Fountain, Jacob at the
Ford," *HUCA* 46 (1975), pp. 33–54.

35 F. Landy has insisted on the ambiguities and the symbolic
character of the Song of Songs in his study, "Beauty and
the Enigma: An Inquiry into some Interrelated Episodes
of the Song of Songs," *JSOT* 17 (1980), pp. 55–106 and
also in *Paradoxes of Paradise . . .*, pp. 137–79 and 318–27.
On polysemy in general, see P. RICOEUR, *La métaphore
vive*, Paris, 1973; S. WITTIG, "A Theory of Multiple
Meanings," *Semeia* 9 (1977), pp. 77–102; ZAHAR SHAVIT,
"The Ambivalence Status of Texts. The Case of Children's Literature," *Poetics Today*, Special Issue Narratol-
ogy: I: Poetic of Fiction, I, 3, Spring 1980, Tel Aviv
University, pp. 75–86. On pluri-isotopy or superposi-
tion of different isotopies in the same discourse, cf. A. J.
GREIMAS and J. COURTES, *Semiotics and Language: an ana-
lytical dictionary*, translated by L. Crist *et al.* (Bloomington: Indiana Univ. Press) 1982, pp. 164 and 236. We
must also mention WALTER H. HERTZBERG, *Polysemy in the
Hebrew Bible* (Ph.D. Dissertation), NYU 1979 (not published). On polyvalence of meanings, cf. R. LAPOINTE, *Les
trois dimensions de l'herméneutique* (Cahiers de la Revue
Biblique, 8), Paris, 1967, p. 33.

CONCLUSION

*A*s A. Robert expressed it, "(There is) no biblical book which has exerted such a seductive influence on the Christian soul as the Song of Songs. Nor has any other so challenged the efforts of interpreters as this short poem."[1] I have attempted to meet that challenge without pretending to have resolved completely all the problems raised by this disconcerting work. I have tried to set it once again in the midst of its historical sources and to search out all its links with the rest of the Bible and also particularly with ancient Egypt. Taking as a starting point the multitude of images and symbols gathered together in the Song, I wanted to emphasize and clarify the propensity of the poet or poets to use allusions and double entendre. Without sacrificing anything of the Hebrew text and without any modification of its consonantal structure, I have proposed some new interpretations that lead to the discovery that the Song is a love poem oriented ultimately toward what was the supreme and invincible hope of the chosen people of the Second Temple period: the coming of the Messiah, at the same time a new David and a new Solomon awaited so anxiously by the daughter of Zion.

But we must definitely maintain as basic to the Song, its radical and essential foundation, the passionate love which draws a man and woman with a mutually inexhaustible and never quenchable thirst. Married love with the opening up of the heart and mind, without any reservation, remains therefore the most expressive symbol of the reciprocal love of Israel and the Messiah, and, in the perspective of the New Covenant, of Christ and the Church. Here as elsewhere in the plan of salvation, grace does not supplant nature, but uplifts and transforms it, even divinizing it.

Therefore we must give up opposing eroticism to allegory,

the natural meaning to the mystical meaning, etc. Here it is question of the eternal reality, both divine and human, of Love. In the beginning God created human beings, in his image, in the unity of a couple: "On the day that God created Adam, he made him in the likeness of God: male and female he created them, blessed them and gave them the name Adam, when they were created" (Gen. 5:1–2; cf. 1:26). Do we have to remind ourselves that the *first* poem in the Bible is a love song: "At last, cried Adam at the sight of Eve, this is bone of my bones and flesh of my flesh" (Gen. 2:23). The Hebrew text then cleverly takes advantage of the untranslatable wordplay between *'îš*, "man," and *'iššâ*, "woman": "This one shall be called woman, for from man was taken this one." This wordplay cannot help but remind us of the wordplay between the name of Solomon and the name of the Shulamite. Starting from such verbal comparisons, very much a technique to aid the memory, the biblical writers endeavored to express the ineffable unity of the human couple, sign and symbol of spiritual realities. The lyrical dialogue between two lovers leads therefore into the mysterious dialogue begun by YHWH with his people, beginning with Abraham, his friend.[2]

The author of the definitive booklet of the Song of Songs must have lived an experience of this kind, as a true son of Abraham. Indeed, this is indicated in his literary work, and, thanks to it, one may sketch his spiritual portrait. Endowed with a keen sensibility and a vivid imagination, a great admirer of the beauties of nature and especially of the human person, he experienced in his own existence what was an intense and deep love. Perfectly familiar with the inspired Scriptures and also with the literatures of neighboring peoples, possessing an open and tolerant mind, he put all his talent at the service of his Jewish brethren in a period of relative tranquility, probably during the fourth century B.C.E. Like his co-religionists, he was especially impatient to see at last the realization of the promises of the Covenant, and the coming of the new David, the new Solomon, the Messiah expected by the people of Israel. He was affected profoundly by the nostalgia for the return of Paradise.[3]

But—and this must be emphasized here—in the oracles of Hosea, Jeremiah, Ezekiel and those of the book of Isaiah, it was question of the loving relationships between God and his people, between YHWH and Israel. In the Song of Songs, we have tried to show that one more threshold has been crossed: from now on it was a question of loving relationships between the Messiah and the daughter of Zion, the new Jerusalem of which the book of Revelation will speak later on (19:7; 21:2ff.).[4] But, in the New Covenant, it is Jesus who is constituted Spouse of the Church of the redeemed, Jews and Gentiles. John the Baptist calls himself friend of the Bridegroom (John 3:29), that is, the groomsman entrusted with seeing that the ceremonies are conducted correctly and especially with ensuring that the bride has carried out the ritual purifications prescribed by the Law.[5] The disciples of Jesus are also called friends of the Bridegroom (Matthew 9:15; Mark 2:19; Luke 5:34). In the parable of the wedding feast (Matthew 22:1ff.), the son of the King is the Messiah. In the parable of the ten virgins (Matthew 25:1ff.), the Bridegroom is Christ. St. Paul brings to mind several times the image of the wedding of Christ and his Church: "I gave you in marriage to a single husband, a virgin pure to present to Christ" (2 Corinthians 11:2). "Husbands, love your wives just as Christ loved the Church: he sacrificed himself for her, to make her holy by purifying her in cleansing water with an accompanying word; for he wished to present her to himself all resplendent, with no speck or wrinkle or anything like that, but holy and faultless" (Ephesians 5:25–27). Human love should be the sign of the love of God for people.

It is only in the light of the New Testament that the Song of Songs has acquired its full meaning. As P. Grelot writes: "The experience of human love, understood and lived according to the norms of biblical revelation, was already transfigured in function of its supernatural archetype, even though the complete revelation of the latter must only be given in the future, at the time when the new covenant would be actualized in a historical fact, when the espousals of God and humanity were accomplished in the incarnation of the Word."[6]

Christian tradition, patristic and medieval, was therefore not mistaken in developing the theme of the wedding of Christ and his Church in regard to the Song of Songs, no matter what may be said of other aspects of the interpretation.[7] Under the multitude of symbols in the language of oriental poetry, the Song reminds us again that God loves us with an eternal love (cf. Jeremiah 31:3).

In his discourse to young people, June 1, 1980, Pope John Paul II told them: "The whole history of humanity is a history of the need to love and be loved." In the Song, it is God himself who recounts this history; he tells us this again today, and tomorrow, and forever. May we know how to listen, may we know how to discover beyond the words, the images, the symbols, the supreme confidence shown in men and women of all times by the One who is Love (1 John 4:8,16). "The Spirit and the Bride say: 'Come!' " (Revelation 22:17).

＊

＊　　＊

---

[1]　ROBERT-TOURNAY, p. 333. St. Augustine had already been of the same opinion: "illa cantica aenigmata sunt" ("the Canticles are enigmas") (Sermon 46:35. *Corpus Christianorum. Series Latina* 41, 1961, p. 560).

[2]　Cf. Is 41:8; 2 Chron. 20:7; Dan. 3:35; James 2:23. In the Ko-

ran, Sura 4, 124, Abraham is called al-Khalil, that is, Friend (of God); this name has become the name of the town of Hebron where the Patriarchs are buried.

3　Cf. F. LANDY, "The Song of Songs and the Garden of Eden," *JBL* 98 (1979), pp. 513–18; there is a longer discussion in *Paradoxes of Paradise . . .* , Chapter 4: "Two Versions of Paradise," pp. 183–265 and 328–58.

4　Cf. A. FEUILLET, "Le Cantique des Cantiques et l'Apocalypse," *RSR* 49 (1961), pp. 321–53.

5　Cf. M.-E. BOISMARD and A. LAMOUILLE, *Synopse des quatre évangiles en français*, vol. III, *L'Évangile de Jean*, Paris, Le Cerf, 1977, p. 127.

6　P. GRELOT, *Le couple humain dans l'Écriture* (Lectio Divina, 31), 1962, p. 71.

7　ROBERT-TOURNAY, p. 26. On the contrary, the Targum and Midrashim as well as the rabbinical commentaries give only a very reduced space to the Messiah. Allegorical interpretation, in Judaism, especially involved the Torah and the history of Israel; cf. R. LOEWE, "Apologetic Motifs in the Targum to the Song of Songs," in *Biblical Motifs: Origins and Transformations*, ed. A. Altmann, Philip W. Lown Institute of Advanced Judaic Studies, Brandeis University, *Studies and Texts*, III (Harvard University Press, 1966), pp. 159–96; POPE, pp. 93ff.; *Shir haShirim, Song of Songs, An Allegorical Translation Based upon Rashi with a Commentary Anthologized from Talmudic, Midrashic and Rabbinic Sources*, commentary compiled by Rabbi Meir Zlotowitz. Allegorical Translation, and Overview, by Rabbi Nasson Scherman. Published by Mesorah Publications, New York, 1977 (Art Scroll Tanach Series). Christian and Jewish commentators confronted one another from the third century onward in regard to the interpretation of the Song of Songs; cf. E. E. URBACH,

"The Homiletical Interpretation of the Sages and the Expositions of Origen on Canticles, and the Jewish-Christian Disputation," *Scripta Hierosolymitana* 22 (1971), pp. 247–75 (translated from the Hebrew of *Tarbiz* 30 (1961), pp. 148–70). In regard to the Targum of the Song of Songs, see E. Z. MELAMED, *Tarbiz* 40 (1971), pp. VI–VII (summary in English).

INDEX I: HEBREW WORDS

172

INDEX II: TEXTS

INDEX III: ANALYTICAL INDEX

BIBLIOGRAPHY

*T*he exhaustive bibliography in M. H. POPE, *Song of Songs* (The Anchor Bible 7C), Garden City, New York: Doubleday, 1977, pp. 233–88 should be consulted. See also the bibliographies in ROBERT-TOURNAY, *Le Cantique des Cantiques* (Études Bibliques), Paris: Gabalda, 1963, pp. 29–39; R. TOURNAY and M. NICOLAŸ, *Le Cantique des Cantiques. Commentaire abrégé*, Paris: Le Cerf, 1967, pp. 183–85; D. LYS, *Le plus beau chant de la création* (Lectio divina 51), Paris: Le Cerf, 1968, pp. 56–60.

The notes after each chapter may be consulted to find references to works published after 1977. Finally, we may draw attention to the following more recent works as a supplementary bibliography on the *Song of Songs:*

B. ARMINJON, *La Cantate de l'Amour; Lecture suivie du Cantique des Cantiques*, Paris: Desclée de Brouwer/Montreal: Bellarmin, 1983.

A. BERLIN, *The Dynamics of Biblical Parallelism*, Bloomington: University of Indiana Press, 1985.

A. BRENNER, "Aromatics and Perfumes in the Song of Songs," *JSOT* 25 (1983), pp. 75–81.

R. COUFFIGNAL, " 'Le glaive et la couronne' Approches nouvelles de Cantique des cantiques, III, 6–11," *Revue Thomiste* 84 (1984), pp. 605–17.

H. DONNER, "Israel und Tyrus in Zeitalter Davids und Salomos; zur gegenseitigen Abhängigheit von Inner- und Aussenpolitik," *Journal of Northwest Semitic Languages* 10 (1982), pp. 43–52.

L. ESLINGER, "The Case of an Immodest Lady Wrestler in Deuteronomy XXV 11–12," *VT* 31 (1981), pp. 269–81 (Song 5:5 would have an erotic double meaning).

M. FALK, *Love Lyrics from the Bible: A Translation and Literary Study of the Song of Songs*, Sheffield: The Almond Press, 1982 (erotic interpretation of the thirty-one poems that make up the Song of Songs).

A. FEUILLET, "Les épousailles messianiques et les références au Cantique des cantiques dans les évangiles synoptiques," *Revue Thomiste* 84 (1984), pp. 181–211; 399–424.

M. FOX, "Scholia to Canticles," *VT* 33 (1983), pp. 199–206.

M. FOX, "Love, Passion and Perception in Israelite and Egyptian Love Poetry," *JBL* 102 (1983), pp. 219–28.

M. FOX, *The Song of Songs and the Ancient Egyptian Love Songs*, Madison: The University of Wisconsin Press, 1985.

G. GARBINI, "La datazione del 'Cantico dei Cantici,' " *Rivista degli Studi Orientali* 56 (1985), pp. 39–46.

C. H. GORDON, "Asymmetric Janus Parallelism," *Eretz Israel* 16 (1982), pp. 80*–81* (a tristich of which the first and third members reflect different senses of the second, as in Song 2:12).

M. GOULDER, *The Song of Fourteen Songs* (*JSOT* Supplement Series 36), Sheffield: The Almond Press, 1986.

G. KRINETZKI, *Kommentar zum Hohenlied; Bildsprache und theologische Botschaft* (Beiträge zur biblischen Exegese und Theologie 16), Frankfurt: P. Lang, 1981.

F. LANDY, "Beauty and the Enigma: An Inquiry into Some Interrelated Episodes of the Song of Songs," *JSOT* 17 (1980), pp.

55–106 (an analysis of sensory, visual, olfactory and tactile imagery, etc.).

F. LANDY, *Paradoxes of Paradise. Identity and Difference in the Song of Songs* (Bible and Literature Series 7), Sheffield: Almond Press, 1983 (reviewed by R. J. Tournay, *RB* 91 (1984), pp. 462–63).

H. MADL, "Dimensionem des Menschen in Israels Lyrik. Von der Stärke der Liebe—wider ihre Verächter (Hoheslied 7,12–8,14)," *Theologie in Dialog. Gesellschaftsrelevanz und Wissenschaftlichkeit der Theologie. Festschrift zum 400-Jahr-Jubiläum der Katholisch-Theologischen Fakultät der Karl-Franzens-Universität in Graz*, Graz: Verlag Styria, 1985, pp. 227–42.

R. MURPHY, "Patristic and Medieval Exegesis—Help or Hindrance?" *CBQ* 43 (1981), pp. 505–16.

R. MURPHY, "Cant. 2, 8–17—A Unified Poem?" *Mélanges bibliques et orientaux en l'honneur de M. Mathias Delcor* (AOAT 215), Kevelaer: Butzon & Bercker / Neukirchen-Vluyn: Neukirchener Verlag, 1985, pp. 305–10.

R. MURPHY, "History of Exegesis as a Hermeneutical Tool: The Song of Songs," *Biblical Theology Bulletin* 16 (1986), pp. 87–91.

F. RAURELL, "Erotic Pleasure in the 'Song of Songs,' " *Laurentianum* 24 (1983), pp. 3–45.

G. RENDSBURG, "Double Polysemy in Genesis 49:6 and Job 3:6," *CBQ* 44 (1982), pp. 48–51.

J. SASSON, "Unlocking the Poetry of Love in the Song of Songs," *Bible Review* 1 (1985), pp. 10–19.

E. WEBSTER, "Patterns in the Song of Songs," *JSOT* 22 (1982), pp. 73–93 (the over-all structure of the Song is chiastic).

N. WYATT, " 'Jedidiah' and Cognate Forms as a Title of Royal Legitimation," *Biblica* 66 (1985), pp. 112–25.